122/4—

# SHIFTING SANDS

To Kristen

best wishes!

Dr. Ruth
Westheimer

ALSO AVAILABLE FROM LANTERN BOOKS
BY DR. RUTH WESTHEIMER AND GIL SEDAN:

*The Olive and the Tree: The Secret Strength of the Druze*

green
press
INITIATIVE

Lantern Books has elected to print this title on Rolland Warm White
a 100% post-consumer recycled paper, processed chlorine-free. As
a result, we have saved the following resources:

42 Trees  (40' tall and 6-8" diameter)
1,986 Gallons of Wastewater
30 million  BTU's of Total Energy
1,986 Pounds of Solid Waste
3,726 Pounds of Greenhouse Gases

As part of Lantern Books' commitment to the environment we
have joined the Green Press Initiative, a nonprofit organization supporting publishers in using fiber that is not sourced from
ancient or endangered forests. We hope that you, the reader, will
support Lantern and the Green Press Initiative in our endeavor
to preserve the ancient forests and the natural systems on which
all life depends. One way is to buy books that cost a little more
but make a positive commitment to the environment not only
in their words, but in the paper that they were published on.
For more information, visit www.greenpressinitiative.org

Environmental impact estimates were made using the Environmental Defense
Paper Calculator. For more information visit: www.papercalculator.org.

# Shifting Sands

*Bedouin Women at the Crossroads*

## DR. RUTH WESTHEIMER
*&*
## GIL SEDAN

Lantern Books • New York

A Division of Booklight Inc.

2009
LANTERN BOOKS
128 SECOND PLACE, GARDEN SUITE
BROOKLYN, NY 11231
www.lanternbooks.com

Cover image of Bedouin women © 2009 by Ruth Westheimer and Gil Sedan:
from the documentary *Shifting Sands* by Ruth Westheimer and Michael
Greenspan; Photos by Michael Greenspan
Design: William Jens Jensen

LIBRARY OF CONGRESS CATALOGING-IN-PUBLICATION DATA

Westheimer, Ruth.
 Shifting sands : the story of Bedouin women in the Negev
/ Ruth Westheimer and Gil Sedan.
    p. cm.
  ISBN-13: 978-1-59056-114-0 (ALK. PAPER)
  ISBN-10: 1-59056-114-7 (ALK. PAPER)
  1. Women—Israel—Negev—History. 2. Women—
Israel—Negev—Social conditions. I. Sedan, Gil. II. Title.
HQ1728.5.W47 2009
305.48'89272056949—dc22
                                                    2008045652

"The strangers who sojourn with you shall be to you as the natives among you, and you shall love them as yourself; for you were strangers in the land of Egypt."

LEVITICUS 19:33–34

# DEDICATION

To the memory of my entire family, who perished during the Holocaust—I am thankful that they had the opportunity to instill in me the much-cherished values of the Jewish Tradition before they were lost to me. And to the memory of my beloved late husband, Manfred Westheimer.

To my wonderful family of now: my daughter Miriam Westheimer, Ed.D., my son-in-law Joel Einleger, MBA, my grandson Ari Einleger, and my granddaughter Leora Einleger; my son Joel Westheimer, Ph.D., my daughter-in-law Barbara Leckie, Ph.D., my granddaughter Michal Westheimer Leckie, and my grandson Benjamin Manfred Westheimer.

# TABLE OF CONTENTS

*Ruth Westheimer and Gil Sedan*

## ACKNOWLEDGMENTS
### BY GIL SEDAN

During my thirty years of work as Arab Affairs Correspondent for Israel Television, I have often traveled to the Negev and met an impressive gallery of residents of the Bedouin community there. However, during this journey with Dr. Ruth Westheimer, I received the deepest insight into the Bedouin community, particularly into the life of Bedouin women, from film director Michael Greenspan and our camera operator Colin Rosin.

As a traditional society, Bedouin culture is rather closed, guarding its secrets tightly. Nevertheless, we were lucky to meet a number of people who opened their hearts and unfolded their most intimate personal stories. Foremost among them were Na'ama and Omar a-Saraya, Mariam abu-Rekayek and Khadra a-San'a, whose personal testimonies occupy much of this book.

Farhan abu-Shleibi, the dynamic entrepreneur of "Desert Ship" in the Negev, impressed us as a genuine link between past traditions and future prospects. Mona al-Habanein of Rahat represented women who dared to challenge their male-dominated society. Qadi Dugan al-Atawneh was kind enough to invite us into the chambers of the religious court in Beersheba and explain to us the complexities of the clash between the law of the desert and the law of the state. Likewise, Sheikh Sami abu-Freh of Rahat impressed us with his attempts to integrate the principles of Islam with the challenges of the modern world, drawing a distinct line between genuine Islam and those who twist Islam for their cynical political ends. Ksenia Svetlova's research illuminated the wider Middle Eastern scene of polygamy, while Prof. Julie Cwikel of Ben-Gurion University in the Negev supplied us with revealing data on the women of the Negev.

Two other remarkable women we met during the work on this book were Rawiya abu-Rabi'a, a lawyer, and Dr. Rania Abedelhadi, a physician. Both young women have long been recognized as pillars of the Bedouin society. Certainly, no story on the Bedouin women in the Negev would be complete without those two distinctive women and their remarkable stories. Their contribution to the welfare and advancement of Bedouin women is indispensable.

We would also like to thank Uri Mintzker, a knowledgeable expert on the Bedouin society, for his constructive remarks on the manuscript. Uri lived with Bedouin tribes in the Negev during his anthropological studies and became their trusted friend, their admirer, and, yes, also their critic. He is currently working on his Ph.D. dissertation on social changes in that society.

However, the main credit in this book is owed to the unknown Bedouin woman who struggles to obtain her rightful place in the society, suffers her share in the plight of the Bedouin society, and bears the torch of change for a better future.

# ACKNOWLEDGMENTS
## BY RUTH K. WESTHEIMER

In 1990, I produced a documentary about the last large migration of Ethiopian Jews to Israel. As someone who has a strong interest in families, I wanted to document how these particular families would adapt to such a drastic change in environment. I followed that documentary with several others on this theme, most recently *The Olive and the Tree*, which is about the Druze living in Israel. During the time I lived in Israel and during my many visits, I was always fascinated by the Bedouin. These nomadic people were slowly settling down in Israel, and I wondered how this change in lifestyle was affecting their culture. Then I learned about a woman who was the first Bedouin woman to become a gynecologist. I recognized that such a historic event meant that major changes were taking place in Bedouin society. Thus, I began to research Bedouin women, and the result was another documentary and this book.

For thousands of years, the Bedouin have been able to adapt to the shifting sands under their feet, but adapting to the sudden shifts in their society is another matter. As a result, I turned to my coauthor and my documentary filmmakers who worked on *The Olive and The Tree* and began the investigation that resulted in this book and the accompanying documentary. We discovered that the changes in opportunity presented in Israel to the Bedouin women are having the greatest effect, far more so than modern conveniences such as electricity. While there are still many young

Bedouin who are struggling to further their education and advance through the ranks of society, the trailblazers who have made it are marking a path that many others will eventually follow, and I want to acknowledge them for their bravery, their energy, their determination, and their contribution to women all over the world.

I join my coauthor in thanking the individuals who helped us make both the film and the book. In addition, I want to add my special thanks to some others who were so vital to this project. As with *The Olive and the Tree,* this project began as a documentary, and it could not have been accomplished without the generous contributions of Retirement Living TV, LLC., The Judy & Michael Steinhardt Foundation, Alan B. Slivka Foundation, Harvey and Constance Krueger, Chicago Foundation for Women, Sylvia Kay Hassenfeld, Sami & Annie Totah Family Foundation, Kenneth & Nira Abramowitz Foundation, Eugene & Estelle Ferkauf Foundation, Washington Hebrew Congregation, and Daniel Carson.

Then there are those who were part of the labor of love that created the documentary, especially Michael Greenspan, who shared executive producer credit with me, wrote the script, directed the filming, and did the narration. Next is Colin Rosin, who produced the film and was our director of photography. Then there's our editor, Hanita Admony-Atoun; the sound people, Misha Spektor and Dani Shaiovitch; the mixer, Eva Spitkovski, from Zinko Studios; graphic designer, Shmuel Gelbard; and online editor, Alon Barak.

Whereas all of the filming took place in Israel, because New York City is my home base, I received a lot of support there as well. Amir Shaviv, Jessica Balaban, and The American Jewish Joint Distribution Committee were instrumental in creating the documentary. Jeffrey E. Tabak, Esq., David Marwell, Ph.D., Daniel Schwartz, MBA, and David

Best, MD, exemplify the support I received from various friends. Cliff Rubin, as my special assistant, kept me organized—no small task. And Pierre Lehu, my Minister of Communications, contributed in so many ways, both in the making of the film and the book that, without him, I don't know if either would have come to pass.

I'd like to acknowledge the hard work of my editors at Lantern Books. Thanks to Gene Gollogly, Martin Rowe, William Jensen, and Kara Davis.

Finally there's my coauthor of this book, Gil Sedan. Gil was my coauthor on *The Olive and the Tree*, and again he brought his contacts and journalistic expertise to the task with enthusiasm and great skill. Gil, again, thank you, thank you, thank you.

❁

During my thirty years of traveling to the land of Israel, in addition to being fascinated by the family life of the Druze, I have become very interested lately in the changing roles of Bedouin women and how those affect their family life. There is a dramatic change that we call shifting sands, because that's where they have lived for centuries—in the sands. The dramatic change is that now women are engaging in occupations that provide a paycheck. I spoke with women who weave products for sale outside of Bedouin society, and with women with post-secondary educations, including a gynecologist and an attorney, with more to come. At the same time, we witnessed a group of women, whom we do not identify, who have tremendous problems in getting the permission from their families and husbands to go to school beyond the eight grade.

What fascinated me was this: What does it do to the fabric of the family when a woman brings home a paycheck, which means that she, too, will have a say in running the house-hold? The difficulties are great, because in such a changing society it is very confusing for a male head of household to adapt to such a change. I saw this difficulty ten years ago, when I did my documentary about the Jews who came from Ethiopia into modern Israel; the women found employment much more quickly than the men did, and we still see some aftermath of those problems. I would like to see more studies of the Bedouin. This documentary and book are intended to raise the issues and stimulate discussions, and now we need more scientific research in this area.

I hope that, in the documentary and in this book, we have provided a way for students and educated readers to gain insight into this issue until further research is forthcoming. For me personally, this was a fantastic learning experience in being able to gain access to and to speak Hebrew with so many Bedouin women. I loved the attorney in blue jeans walking in the market with me and telling me, "Dr. Ruth, you see on the outside I look like everybody else; in the inside, I'm a Bedouin woman, and I will remain a Bedouin woman."

Finally, to all those women who have the courage to change, to adapt to new realities in Israel, I wish you all the very best, and I promise to visit again.

# INTRODUCTION

I magine that you undergo a dramatic change in your life, that after years of happy childhood in the countryside, you are abruptly uprooted from this comfortable hotbed of fresh air, starlit nights, early mornings with the call of roosters and endless corn fields, and transplanted into the middle of Manhattan and told that this is your new home, no way to turn the wheel back. That's it, the good old days are over and gone; this is your new life, and, mind you, you had better like your good life, because someone else—that omnipotent force that uprooted you—is absolutely convinced that your new life is good for you.

Now imagine that you know that this good life is *not* good for you, and that in reality your new life serves only the interests of the powerful force that now enjoys your corn fields, your roosters, and your star-filled skies.... Moreover, imagine that there is nothing you can do about it because, no matter what, that brutal force is a hundred times stronger than you are.

Now this is, more or less, what has been happening to the Bedouin population in Israel, which in the past sixty years was forced to relinquish its nomadic life, give up absolute rule of the desert, and move to permanent homes that they have not chosen and that they absolutely detest.

Throughout most of their history, the Bedouin were the nomads of the deserts in the Middle East, wandering from place to place in search of water and grazing for their herds, striking roots in the family and in the tribe, living in makeshift tents, never on a defined piece of land. It was their tradition that has kept them going in these harsh surroundings, their key to survival, and in the heart of that tradition was the Bedouin honor—the honor of religion, the land, and the woman. These three should never be compromised. And the family is cherished most.

Bedouin are family people. The family is the glue that holds them together. Now, however, as Bedouin throughout the Middle East are undergoing changes, the family, too, is no longer what it used to be. The clash between modern life and centuries-old traditions make these changes unavoidable. And no changes are more dramatic than those undergone by the Bedouin population in Israel, an Arab traditional society in the midst of a modern, Western-oriented Jewish state.

The Bedouin population in Israel is divided between the northern group in the Galilee, who are descended from tribes that emigrated from Syria, and the southern tribes, who came originally from Sinai and the Arabian Peninsula. Both groups have been transformed from nomadic tribes to semi-urban and semi-rural communities ever since the establishment of the State of Israel in 1948.

In the old days, the vast expanses of the Bedouin desert knew no limits, and the Bedouin roamed free; but the establishment of the State of Israel changed all that, and introduced Western concepts of civic order, which left no room for nomads. In the eyes of the authorities, government officials were now the landlords of the desert, and their subjects would have to settle down, and that included the Bedouin. They were forced to fold down their tents and move to new townships.

The move has radically affected the Bedouin, and sent tremors throughout that traditional society—tremors that only get stronger.

This book deals with some hundred and seventy thousand Bedouin who live in Israel's Negev desert, a minority within the large Arab minority (some twenty percent) in the Jewish state. We were fascinated by the rapid changes that the Bedouin society has witnessed in the past six decades, and particularly by the challenges to their tradition of family life. Bedouin women are affected most by those changes but, of course, they in turn affect the lives of Bedouin men.

For centuries on end, the Bedouin were among the more conservative societies in the world, and suddenly—bang!—drastic and rapid changes. Those changes amount to a real revolution, albeit a gradual, painful one. The torch-bearers of that revolution are without doubt the Bedouin women. They are not there yet, but a thorough look reveals the buds of an imminent revolution among the Bedouin women in Israel's south. There are growing signs that young women increasingly refuse to accept the rules imposed upon them by society still dominated by men.

This book will tell the story of the Bedouin women in Israel, their harsh realities, and their flamboyant pioneers, who are gradually breaking down the walls of generations of tradition to free themselves from ancient shackles.

This is the story of the Desert Revolution.

*The Negev desert in Israel*

# THE BEDOUIN IN ISRAEL

When the sun rises over the Bedouin village of Bir-Hadaj—or for that matter any Bedouin settlement in the Negev desert—its rays seem to touch the most serene place in the world. A Bedouin village is an island of tranquility, a sharp contrast to the ever-busy modern-day life, which can be witnessed only a few kilometers away, in the Jewish town of Beersheba, the capital of the Negev.

The day begins early in Bir-Hadaj. The villagers rise to the croaking of roosters; women rush to prepare breakfast in improvised kitchens hidden in black tents or tin shacks; children cling desperately to last minutes of sleep; and men get ready to leave for work. Rising early has been a Bedouin practice for generations. In the past, when they had no electricity, they wanted to make the best of every minute of daylight. Even so, they took it easy; it was life in slow motion; nobody rushed anywhere.

Most Bedouin would have liked it to stay that way. They want to continue life as it has been for generations, without the interference and temptations of the outside world. They like it slow, traditional—and patriarchal. This is why most Bedouin men are the strongest lobby for *no* change. They are the ones who would lose the most. The women can only gain.

Some twenty miles north of Bir-Hadaj, one can witness yet another Bedouin island of the past. The Bedouin market in Beersheba looks like a scene transplanted from a marketplace in Gaza or perhaps even in a remote Sahara Desert village. Only the skyline of high-rise apartment complexes of Jewish Beersheba spoils the picturesque desert scene.

Early Thursday morning, minivans loaded with sheep fill a large plot of rough terrain at the southern end of the city. After they unload the cattle, the Bedouin gather in small groups and haggle over their sheep. Most wear the traditional dark *abaya* robes. Cars and skyline excluded, the same scene has repeated itself for generations. Here, too, time seems to have stood still.

Many of the Bedouin men stand idly by their cars, waiting for a customer to show up. Business has not been good recently. Ever since Israel closed the borders with Gaza and the West Bank, their best customers—the brothers across the Green Line—no longer come, and prices have plummeted.

The traditional livestock market is gasping for life. For generations, Bedouin from all over the Negev have come here to do business, to show off their wealth of sheep and goats—and to see one another. This used to be the *agora* of the desert, but no more. The silence of the lamb and their

*Bedouin market, Beersheba, Israel*

owners. Yes, many can show off the latest models of jeeps and pickup trucks, but the market has lost its grandeur, which has been so symbolic of the Bedouin situation in general. They have lost their ancient heritage, with nothing to fill in the gap.

Indeed, the Bedouin population is caught at a crossroads. As they increasingly adopt a contemporary lifestyle—with modern utilities and sanitation, medical care, educational and economic opportunities—Israeli Bedouin are hard-pressed to preserve their unique heritage and cultural integrity. They are struggling to retain their "people-hood." As a matter of bon ton, most Bedouin declare allegiance to the good old slow and conservative way of life, but the high-rise buildings of Beersheba and taste of the "free" Jewish pattern of life are tempting.

Shehadeh abu-Sbeit, a school principal, told us, "If I respect Bedouin tradition, than I will be respected; but if I despise it, the entire society will despise me. All children, boys and girls alike, now dress modern; they want to go to the mall, they want their parents to own a new car, they appreciate money and luxury items, and all of this is against Bedouin tradition."

Indeed, this is a very difficult choice. Most Bedouin would like to taste the best of both worlds. They want to free themselves from some of the old shackles, yet they are afraid that if they become too Western, they might not only lose the bonds of tradition, but also create irreparable cracks in their own families. Therefore, they choose the in-between, the compromise, often losing out.

The women lose the most. The men can afford jumping from one end of the spectrum to another. The women cannot. Their male-dominated society is intolerant of "advanced" women. Unless they enjoy the support of their father and brothers, they will be very lonely in their battle.

Often unaccepted by their Jewish neighbors and on a perpetual collision course with the authorities, the Bedouin have created their own "autonomy"—some forty-six "unrecognized" villages. The villages were erected in places that the tribes claim as their territory from ancient times; others were simply chosen as a matter of convenience, for their proximity to water sources or because internal conflicts forced families to depart from the main tribe and seek an alternative place, away from the tribal storm.

Frequently, such villages were located out of reach of the authorities, but are nevertheless threatened by police raids, reinforced by teams of bulldozers that have demolished hundreds of "illegal" Bedouin houses, huts, and tin homes. The complex of Bedouin townships, recognized and unrecognized, has created what some call "Bedouinland," south of Beersheba. Aerial photos of that region create the impression that the Bedouin have taken over this part of the Negev desert. The catch, however, is that Bedouin "autonomy" has grown wild. Many so-called unrecognized villages are deprived of basic government services, including electricity, regular water supply, and health and education services. Some forty percent of those villagers are not connected to the national water system.

In the past, the tribe's elders were the law; and tribal law was just as effective, if not even more so, than the state law. However, one consequence of modern life was the diminishing influence of the sheikhs and the elders in the family. The younger generation, particularly the boys, lack respect for the elderly; they often disobey their parents and do what they please. This is the background for growing crime rates among the Bedouin in the Negev, second in intensity only to the crime rate in metropolitan Tel-Aviv.

Nevertheless, as a general rule, the Negev police usually stay out of those villages. They have adopted a practice of trying to avoid conflict—except when the Israel Land Administration and the interior ministry send them on surprise raids designed to demolish illegal housing. Bedouin criminals have turned their "autonomy" into hideouts by taking advantage of the situation, and law-abiding citizens have often paid the price.

Parts of "Bedouinland" have become hubs for crimes such as drug trafficking from Sinai, trade in women (mostly women from the former Soviet Union, who are "sold" into prostitution in Israel), a prospering market of stolen cars, and at times connections with terrorist organizations in the occupied territories. With no law enforcement agency in sight, only in Bedouin villages can children under the age of ten drive cars.

Many Bedouin often perceive their Jewish neighbors as the favored, spoiled child who unjustly receives various benefits from mother government, whereas the Bedouin are discriminated against and deprived of basic rights such as equal appropriation of land and water. Thus, the Jewish neighbor is often considered a legitimate target for theft, and Jewish businesspeople are often subject to violent extortion.

The majority of law-abiding Bedouin—those who seek a stable framework of life—do not trust the state-sponsored framework. Many turn to the Islamic Movement, which provides them with kindergartens, social services, and mosques—many mosques. This is interesting, since Bedouin society in the past was not religious in the ordinary sense of the word.

By the end of the first decade of this century, the Bedouin of the Negev will have had almost no independent economic basis. Most of them have worked as unskilled and cheap laborers for Jewish employers. This problem has worsened as the authorities have taken measures to abolish the traditional Bedouin economy, which consists of herding and small-scale, primitive agriculture. The ministry of agriculture has limited the size of their herds and their grazing territory and has refrained from subletting land to them for significant periods of time.

The size of "Bedouinland" has created concern in the government—and fear among Jewish settlers in the south—that the Bedouin are taking over the Negev. But are they? Although by 2008 the Bedouin population in the Negev constituted some twenty-three percent of the total

population, their settlements had spread only to one percent of the land. Whereas the average allotment of land in
the Bedouin settlements was .185 acres per person, in the
Jewish towns it stood at 0.7 acres per person, almost four
times as much. Whereas, in the Negev Bedouin township
of Tel-Sheva, some ten thousand people live in an area of
one thousand acres, a Jewish single-family farm controls
fifteen hundred acres.

The Bedouin feel that the state has forced them into
a planning framework that contrasts with their reality
and their desires. The result of this process is turning a
significant part of the Bedouin population from a semi-
nomadic, rural population into urban communities that
lack economic resources and are troubled with a multitude
of socioeconomic problems. Consequently, the Bedouin
have developed strong feelings of loss, discrimination,
and alienation toward the state. The Bedouin have been
limited in their settlements, and very few have been fortunate enough to own their own farms. The Israel Land
Administration—a powerful government agency that
runs all state-owned land—has not leased land to the
Bedouin. On the other hand, in recent years the state has
authorized thirty private farms to Jewish farmers, who
control thousands of acres.

Indeed, the land dispute between the Bedouin and
the authorities has marred relations between this fragile
Arab minority and the Jewish state. Back in the 1970s, the
Bedouin claimed 200,000 acres in the Negev as their own,
but by the turn of the century the government insisted
that the Bedouin were entitled to live in and cultivate only
90,000 acres. The rest has been under legal dispute, far

*A Bedouin "unrecognized" dwelling*

from being resolved, while, relations between the Bedouin and the authorities have only worsened.

The settlement process of the nomadic Bedouin population really began during the British Mandate, and was accelerated after 1948, when Israel took over the Negev in its War of Independence. Thus, we can trace the roots of the conflict back to the early days after that war. At first, the Bedouin's encounter with the Jews was positive. The Bedouin believed that the Jews would bring progress. The Jews, on the other hand, believed that the Bedouin would teach them the secrets of the desert.

Some 110,000 Bedouin lived in the Negev on the eve of Israel's establishment. When war broke out and an Egyptian army invaded the Negev and confronted the young Jewish army, the Bedouin fled to Sinai and Jordan, leaving only ten thousand behind. Unfortunately, the Jews perceived the Bedouin as a potential enemy, thus the young state limited Bedouin movement, encouraged them to leave, and the Bedouin trauma became part of the overall Palestinian *Nakba*—the Arabic term for the Palestinian "catastrophe" of 1948.

By and large, the Bedouin population in the Negev had no problem accepting the authority of the new Jewish state, as long as they were free to roam the desert. However, during the early 1950s, the State of Israel limited the Bedouin into a concentrated area called the Sayag. They were allowed to leave only by special permission of the military government. Entire tribes were displaced from their lands in the western and southern Negev and transferred to the Sayag area. The state zoned much of the Sayag area for agriculture, and building was forbidden. Thus, every permanent building that was erected—some were only wooden and tin huts—was considered illegal, and their inhabitants became law-breakers.

The State of Israel believed they could solve the problem by forcing the Bedouin into newly-built townships, whose character contrasted sharply with their traditional way of life. We will soon discuss this issue at length, since it has been a major contributor to the Desert Revolution.

This was the state of affairs in the summer of 2007, when we traveled to the Negev to become acquainted with the Bedouin population. We spoke to dozens of men and women, young and old, educated and less educated, until we could form a picture of that fragile yet determined community, friendly yet angry, hopeful but lamenting. Today, the Bedouin of the Negev live in thirteen townships; half of the people still inhabit the "unrecognized villages." Once again, there is much talk about a government plan to resolve the land dispute in a way that would put an end to their miserable life. Unfortunately, there is too much talk—and paper work—while too little is actually being done.

This is the way they live, make their living, raise children, and build hope for the future. It is in this environment that the women play a particularly difficult role.

## RECOGNIZED AND UNRECOGNIZED

Throughout the years, the government has used various tactics to deal with the Bedouin population in the Negev. First they tried to scare them off across the border, then they restricted them to the Sayag area, and then they tried the townships. After the military government that oversaw Israel's Arab population was lifted in 1964, the Bedouin spread throughout the Negev, at times returning to their original places, at times seeking new grounds.

By the late 1960s, the government finally realized that they could not prevent unplanned and disorganized Bedouin building without providing a decent alternative. Their new idea was to build seven townships. The logic behind that idea was their hope that the townships would be so attractive that Bedouin from all over the Negev would flock into the towns and set aside their nomadic habits. Yet there was a problem; the townships were called Bedouin towns. This involved an inherent contradiction, since towns are exactly the opposite to the natural Bedouin habitat—the desert. Indeed, the authorities hardly consulted the Bedouin before they set up the townships. Living conditions in the townships contrasted sharply with the traditional Bedouin way of life. For centuries on end, the Bedouin had been the kings of the desert; they considered the entire desert their

*A Bedouin herding sheep*

home and moved from place to place according to water resources and grazing lands.

So how did the authorities convince them to abandon their centuries-old way of life in favor of the townships? First, they offered comfortable loans to those Bedouin who were ready to build homes in the new towns. Second, they adopted a tough policy toward the Bedouin who refused to play along.

The township option did not quite work out, however. Many Bedouin refused to move to the townships and make their homes on their original sites of residence or wherever had been deemed suitable. By 2008, the Bedouin population in the Negev was divided between those who were unhappy living in townships, on the one hand, and on the other (also unhappy), those living in unrecognized villages that lack basic state services.

The government had partially tried to solve the conflict in 2003 by recognizing yet another group of seven Bedouin settlements. Nevertheless, the problem remains. According to the Regional Council for Unrecognized Villages in the

Negev, by 2008, close to half of the population still lived in the "unrecognized" villages. Official policy is uncompromising; government officials claim there is "no chance" that the state will recognize illegal communities. The reasons cited are conveniently economic rather than political, thus trying to eliminate any allegations of racial discrimination. According to the government, the state cannot set up roads, water, electricity, and sewage for any families that have decided to settle a remote spot in the desert; neither can it draw up master plans for groups of a few hundred people.

To cope with the phenomenon of illegal building and the uncontrolled spread of Bedouin settlements in the Negev, the government adopted a tough policy of demolishing houses, destroying crops, confiscating herds of sheep and goats, and denying basic services such as water, electricity, access roads, schools, clinics, and sewage systems to Bedouin who lived in "unrecognized villages."

"We used to live in tents," recalled Ali a-Saraya, sixty-three. He lives with his family in wooden huts near the town of Arad. "We used to ride our camels from the town of Rahat [just north of Beersheba] all the way to Arad [a Jewish town at the eastern part of the Negev]. Now we are using cars and tractors. We used to walk hours on end with our sheep, walking during the day and sleeping in the field, no one had bothered us."

With years of drought in the Negev, there is a growing gap between the supply of and demand for grazing fields for the sheep. Bedouin shepherds thus wander with their sheep up to the northern plateau, which is richer in greenery. They stay out in the fields from February until May—until the grazing period is over—and then spend the summer in their huts near Arad.

"Today, when we stay with the sheep in the north for three or four days longer, they say our permit time is over. In the past there was freedom; now there isn't. Why? Because, in the past, the government did not mind the Bedouin. I am trying to build houses for the children, but once I begin with construction work, they say this is not your own land and prevent me from building. This way, they force me to buy a house in the town, but I cannot live there because I lived all my life in tents."

Although the state has described Bedouin movement into the townships as a way of upgrading their standard of living, many Bedouin perceive this as just the opposite, as a means of forcing them to increase their expenses.

Ali: "Living in the town, I need more money than I have. Out in the wilderness, I lived in a tent made of goat wool, which protected us against the wind, the cold, and the rain. I used to buy two sacks of flour a month, I collected twigs, I put up a fire and I had a meal; but in the town you need gas, electricity, and if I light up a bonfire, the neighbors protest."

When the officials spell out their official policy, they sound quite assertive and determined, but the truth is that the authorities are quite helpless. They do not really know how to cope with the situation, which continues to worsen. There is no real comprehensive master plan to solve the problem once and for all. In addition, the existing plans are only partial and too slow, creating a growing gap between the challenges and futile attempts to solve them.

The state is aware of the problem, not only of the Bedouin themselves, but also of the overall development of the Negev.

*Ali a-Saraya*

So far, however, it has not found a way to cope with these problems in a systematic way. It cannot force some hundred and seventy thousand people to change their entire way of life and move into properly run urban centers, yet the state has not figured out a way to convince the Bedouin to do it by consent. Indeed, the Bedouin in the "diaspora" put up a stiff fight. Refusing to move to the townships, they insist on their rights as Israeli citizens to receive the basic services, of which they have been deprived. Moreover, their situation worsens daily. Only after public and legal struggles has the government been obliged to build twenty regional schools and eight clinics for these unrecognized villages, as well as to connect some of the villages to the water system.

The townships have been a failure from every point of view, except for the official view of the government. The townships have remained pockets of unemployment and welfare assistance, blighted by problems of hard crime and violence, and suffering from a dearth of employment, public transportation, banks, larger businesses, industrial zoning, and, worst of all, basic infrastructure.

Sheikh Sami abu-Freh is the Imam, the master of prayers, at one of the mosques in the township of Rahat, some ten miles north of Beersheba. He lives in a modern villa at the edge of town, with a car and two camels parked outside; and yet he is not content with life. We entered the premises through a small gate in the wall that led to the entrance of the house. Behind the house was a small animal farm, a few horses, two camels, and a few chickens—a living monument to the days when Bedouin assets were measured in terms of camels and horses instead of the currency of agorot and shekels.

Dressed in his white *abaya*, Sheikh abu-Freh invited us into his office, a small air-conditioned room with walls covered by loaded book shelves. Most of the books were on religion and Bedouin law, the law of the desert. The office was well-equipped, with a computer and a printer—the office of present-day man of religion.

Sami's wife, a teacher of literature and religion at the local high school, made a short appearance, offered cold drinks and fruit, and disappeared into another room. The presence of another woman in the room—Dr. Ruth—was not a good enough reason for Sheikh Sami to invite his wife to stay. The presence of other men in the room was a good enough reason to make her stay away.

Abu-Freh served us the short, bitter Bedouin coffee. We drank politely, suddenly feeling the urge for a decent

cappuccino but, to honor the sheikh of the house, saying nothing. While pouring coffee, abu-Freh offered us
an instant guide to Bedouin coffee customs. He will offer
his male guest only a partly filled *finjan,* or coffee cup,
and then keep half-filling it until the guest says *"ammar,"*
a definite "no more, thank you." The woman guest, on
the other hand receives only one full cup (*finjan ajouz,* or
*"finjan* for the old woman").

"How does one find the balance between tradition and
modern life? It is not easy. You look at this room and you
say to yourself, here is a modern Bedouin, a happy Bedouin,
content with modern life and its comforts. Wrong. I am not
a happy Bedouin. I have not adjusted to this room and this
way of living, because I did not choose it. Someone made
the choice for me. I feel imprisoned in my own home. I still
miss the nomadic life in the desert. I dream of the day that I
wake up in the land of my grandparents, without books and
running water, without a brick shelter over my head—but as
a free person. Free to live my life the way I want to live it."

Sheikh Sami said he had deliberately built his home at
the far end of town, away from the city-like hustle, where
he enjoys the illusion of a farm, with horses and camels
"where I can taste a little of long-gone freedom."

We heard similar comments wherever we went in the
Negev. In particular, many of those who expressed their
longing for the "primitive" past were young, educated, and
successful Bedouin who lacked nothing of the comforts of
life. From our point of view, they, too, should be content
with their lives and should have nothing to complain about.

Shehadeh abu-Sbeit, a school principal, in his early fif-
ties, told us, "We didn't know how to combine the noblesse

of Bedouin life and the positive elements of modern life. My generation is a bridge between tradition and modern life. However, in my capacity as a principal, I sometimes neglect tradition. I cannot appear with a traditional dress in school, when all the kids are dressed modernly and speak about their visits to the shopping mall. There was a time when I was totally pro-modernization. I thought progress was good and that it should be attained at all cost; but now I realize that I cannot detach myself from Bedouin tradition, even if I am a doctor from the Sorbonne."

Shehadeh was a guest we met at a festive luncheon in the woods offered by Omar a-Saraya, one of our hosts during our Bedouin journey. As he spoke, he looked around at the guests seated on cushions and enjoying their meals. "Imagine I would ask the people seated here on carpets to get me a chair; why, they would either laugh at me or excommunicate me. I want to feel my Bedouism. If I keep tradition, everyone will respect me. This will only reinforce my social standing. If I despise Bedouism, the entire society will despise me. This is not an easy choice. I feel a tremendous difficulty to be both an authentic Bedouin and a modern Israeli; however one manipulates, one comes on account of the other. One cannot be a true Bedouin and an enlightened Israeli—the way the Israelis would like me to be."

Jaber abu-Shleibi helps his older brother Farhan run a Bedouin tourist village, south of Beersheba. On the face of it, he is an advanced young Bedouin, and yet Jaber, like many other young Bedouin, sticks to traditional values and longs for the simplicity of the past, when all the comforts of present-day life did not exist: "I went with a friend to watch *Charlie's Angels* at a cinema in Beersheba. I did not understand what the big deal was. Cinema paralyzes you, shuts your brains, and turns you into a nonentity. I would rather sit and listen to the silence of the desert, to the cries of the wolves."

People like Sheikh Sami abu-Freh and Jaber abu-Shleibi do not really dream of a remote tent in the desert. They are not really willing to give up the basic comforts of a modern, Western lifestyle. However, if it had been up to them, the Bedouin residents of the Negev could have built up their own villages in the area they used to control. In this way, they would enjoy both the benefits of modern services and the links to ancient heritage.

Hussein a-Rafayah, a resident of one of the unrecognized villages, told us, "This has been our land for generations. Turkey had left, then England, then came Israel. At first, Israel left everyone on his land, and then the demolitions came. The state does not want you to build except in a registered plot in the townships."

Indeed, during 2007, the state demolished hundreds of "illegal" Bedouin constructions. Moreover, for years, the Israel Land Administration sent light airplanes to spray Bedouin fields with chemicals, which was a punitive measure against alleged illegal seizure of land. However, when the High Court of Justice ruled that the spraying itself was illegal, the state opted for tractors that ploughed and turned over land before the Bedouin could pick the crops.

Here is an example of the gap between the state's perception of the Bedouin's problems and the Bedouin's own perception: The state treats all the Bedouin of the Negev as one parcel. However, the Bedouin make a strict distinction between their family and their tribe on the one hand, and

*An "unrecognized" Bedouin settlement*

the state on the other hand. Thus, when the state urges several Bedouin tribes to settle in a township in an area that had once belonged to another tribe, the state faces resistance that has nothing to do with the natural objection to permanent housing, but has everything to do with the delicacies of intertribal relations. "I am not willing to move to another territory, and then find myself confronting the original owners of that land, claiming that I have trespassed on their territory, because that means asking for trouble," said Hussein a-Rafayah.

Life in the unrecognized villages is difficult for the simple reason that many do not receive basic state services. "We suffer from heat and cold; there is no electricity; and we need to deliver water with a container from the nearby township of Lagiya."

*Would you like to build a permanent house?* "I want to build a house, just like everyone else. But we are not willing to move to another place. We must stay on our land, because, if we move to other lands, there will be violence. I would love to enjoy the comforts of modern life, but in my own home, on my own land, not at someone else's place."

The Arab citizens of Israel are exempt from military service because of the delicate situation in which "their state is in conflict with their people," in the words of former Arab leader Abdul Aziz Zuabi. Although they were not expected to do army service, many young Bedouin volunteered for service, partly because this was a way of an additional income to the family. In recent years, however, the number of Bedouin volunteers has shrunk because of diminishing motivation and growing feelings of alienation toward the state. "Our son may go into the army, and yet the state may demolish our house."

*What do you think of those who moved to the townships?* "People who move don't own their own land. This is different from us land owners. I want to have my old land back; that's why I am not willing to leave."

Thus, the conflict between the state and the Bedouin population is not merely about land and shekels but also the result of a gap in culture. Elements such as land and tribal honor, the pillars of Bedouin culture, are simply ignored by the state. For the state, a Bedouin is a Bedouin is a Bedouin.

According to Qadi Dugan al-Atawneh, judge of the religious court in Beersheba, "Unfortunately, the state has so many problems that it does not find the time and the energy to deal with the problem of the Bedouin population. Governments change; ministers change; and the Bedouin remain the weak population. They need assistance, but the state does not help. Thus the vacuum created entails so many problems."

As one travels farther south, the whole desert scene looks detached from the rest of Israel. Vast stretches of land are covered with tin houses, huts, and tents—shanty villages shared among humans and animals, sometimes with no regular settlement in sight. It is the Negev sheikhdom, a state within a state—unable to stand on its own feet, unable to come to terms with the lawful state. Situation impossible.

## BOYS AND GIRLS

*"I love women, but according to our religion I cannot take a girl from the side, so I marry another one. And don't you raise your eyebrows—you Jews can have three girls from the side, as long as nobody knows about it."*

— HUSSEIN A-RAFAYAH in a moment of truth

Hussein a-Rafayah, in his mid-fifties, wears the traditional black *abaya* and a white *kafiye*—yet another expression of his devotion to Bedouin heritage. The Bedouin *abaya*, or *thobe*, is the main body covering for men, which is an ankle-length shirt, often tailored with cuffs, a collar, two side pockets and a breast pocket. However, the most easily recognized aspect of a Bedouin's attire is the headgear, which consists of the *kafiye*, cloth, and *'agal*, black rope, which is indicative of the wearer's ability to uphold the obligations and responsibilities of manhood.

"I cannot ignore my Bedouin way of life; neither do I want to change it," said Hussein. "Some young Bedouin wear modern, Western-style attire, but the real Bedouin cannot change. A Bedouin will never change. He will always remain Bedouin, wherever he lives."

*Hussein a-Rafayah*

Although, according to the Qur'an, the woman is considered equal to the man, in practice, the woman in the traditional Bedouin society is clearly a second-class citizen. Even the way she dresses indicates the proscriptions of tradition. They, too, wear the gown, usually black, which does not flatter their femininity. While all women are required to keep their hair covered, married women in particular wrap a black cloth, known as *'asaba*, about their forehead. In recent years, with the growing influence of Islam, more and more young women turn to the traditional attire, although one can still see young women in modern dress, like any other Western woman.

The Bedouin society is a patriarchal, male-dominant society. The man is the boss in the family. The father has the ultimate say regarding family affairs, and all family members—without exception—must obey him.

The father is considered the absolute ruler; his sons are the princes; the wives and the daughters are his obedient subjects. An older brother will tell his sisters what to do, will escort her outside the tribe's limits and, at times, might even kill her if he feels that she has betrayed family honor. Once a Bedouin boy turns to become a husband, he, in his turn, will take control of the family—first over his wife, then over his children.

From early childhood, the tribe and the family design different paths for the boy and the girl. The girl—and later the woman—is limited to the home. The boy, as long as he lives with his parents, has the mandate to look after family affairs according to the rules of his father. Once he is married, he is free to do as he pleases. This obvious discrimination against women is the fuel for the Bedouin feminine revolution.

"In the Bedouin society, the woman finds herself at the bottom of the totem pole," said women's rights activist Mona al-Habanein. "She comes after the parents, the grandparents, and the brothers. Even her own sons are considered superior to her. If a member of the family tortures her or bothers her, she will not talk. She is discriminated against by her husband, the family, the society, and the establishment. Everybody dominates her. I have heard of women all over the world, but I have yet to see women who are worse off than the Bedouin woman."

The man is the head of the family. He is the one who decides on all family matters—certainly about the fate of the women in the family. His wife (or wives, as we shall see) cannot cross the border of her traditional role as a homemaker and mother without the consent of the family head and his obedient servants, the male children. The woman cannot leave home, study, or work without the consent of the husband. She cannot become part of his social life beyond the realm of the immediate family. When the head of the family receives male guests, she may wait on them, but she will not stay in the room.

Separation between men and women is paramount in *all* social events.

The family is part of the overall tribal structure, which gives the tribe's elderly the authority to run tribal affairs. In short, Bedouin individuals must give precedence to tribal and family interests over their own interests. This is particularly true of the woman. The good news is that things are changing.

In the past sixty years, Bedouin society in Israel has undergone a process of gradual urbanization. As a result, it has lost some of its collective solidarity. The rapid urbanization and modernization process has weakened the role of tradition and changed the role of young people in the Bedouin society, particularly that of women. All the Bedouin women we have met have paid respect to tradition and tribal values. Nevertheless, it is a fact that, as society becomes less traditional, women gain more independence. The process is gradual, has its ups and downs, but the destination is clear: compared to the role of the woman in Bedouin society just twenty years ago, this is indeed a revolution, albeit so far a slow one.

The division of family responsibilities is clear, according to Ali a-Saraya, an elderly Bedouin who was kind enough to explain the Bedouin facts of life. The women run the house, and it is the husband's duty to supply the means. "I work outside, they work at home." As a general rule, the husband will go to the market, buy food, clothes, and furniture; the woman will cook, feed the children (and the animals), prepare them for school, clean the house, and do the laundry.

"The woman cannot do whatever she pleases," Ali a-Saraya told us. "She cannot go chattering all day, blah

blah blah blah; this is not good. The woman belongs in the tent; that is her responsibility. It is not her job to take money and go to the market shopping. The clothes—that is for the woman; the children—that is for the woman; the wash—that is for the woman; the food—that is for the woman, food only a woman. All the rest should be left for the men."

With the girls at home, the oldest daughters are always expected to help in preparing the meals, while the younger girls are responsible for gathering all the needed ingredients. As the mother prepares the food, her daughters are expected to stay in the cooking section and learn the art of cooking.

All other house duties—whatever is left—are the husband's responsibility. Ali a-Saraya tells us, "When the children are naughty, she [my wife] will tell me, and I will reprimand the child. The girl must first listen to her father and brothers, only then to her mother. I will not consent to my wife driving. I do not know what she does on the way. The girl must behave properly; she is not free to speak to any man, and she cannot go wherever she pleases. If she goes to the doctor, she must be accompanied by a man. However, if a woman has no husband or children, she may have no choice but to go alone to the market.

"Unfortunately, nowadays, the women no longer behave properly. This is something that my sons, too, should take into account. Suppose your son goes to town and speaks to a girl. Her father might regard this as an act of disrespect. This could create war. A girl must behave politely. If someone talks badly to her, she should keep silence. She must ignore him and report to her father, husband, or brothers. It is their duty to take care of the matter.

"Yesterday, two women from our village met my son Ahmad in the township of Lagiya and asked him for a ride home. But he refused, because if he took them, the father or brother could ask, *Why did you take them?*, and this would create a conflict. He might even kill the girl. This is a matter of honor."

The Bedouin population in Israel's south is caught in a peculiar situation. It lives in proximity of the Western-oriented, relatively liberal Israeli society and is affected by it. On the other hand, it is a deeply traditional society. This creates an internal tension, which is expressed most dramatically in the role of the women in Bedouin society.

This order of life has been changing in recent years. Bedouin girls go to school, some continue on to the university. The more educated they become, the greater their opposition to the male-dominated society. Many go out to work. Thus, in some educated Bedouin families, the women are (almost) equal partners, very much as they are in the surrounding Jewish environment. However, this applies to a very small minority. In addition, this minority, for the first time ever, goes out to work and returns with a paycheck. And just like anywhere else in the world, money means power. For the first time in Bedouin history, the man must share power with the woman, and this creates a revolution—a drastic change in the traditional role of the women.

Prof. Julie Cwikel and Nurit Barak, researchers of the Bedouin society, have suggested that the society has divided the life of the Bedouin woman into three stages.[1] In the first stage, from the age of ten until just before marriage, the girl's social status is low, and her function in life is to help her mother at home and with the herds. Socially, she

*Dr. Rania Abedelhadi*

can befriend only other girls in the tribe. Before marriage, contact with any men beyond the immediate family circle is absolutely forbidden to assure her virginity on the wedding night.

During the second stage, after marriage, her social contacts expand, and she gets to associate with both her family and her husband's family. The ideal woman will bear many children, preferably boys. Such a woman gains the appreciation and respect of her family. A woman who bears only girls is considered of a lower status, and is more likely to face another wife in the family.

The third stage, after menopause: If she is the mother of boys, she will rely on their strength. She is even allowed to meet with men at the home when her husband and children are away from home. Her authority in the home expands, and she is in charge of the household. Her daughters-in-law must obey her. However, if she is only a mother to children, her status is once again low, and her social contacts are limited as well.[2]

"I am very sorry to say that, even when you ask educated men, they often believe the woman is inferior to them," Dr. Rania Abedelhadi told us. She is the first Bedouin woman physician, one of the torch-bearers of the Desert Revolution. "Men often quote the Qur'an to substantiate this argument, but this is a misinterpretation of the ban on women's prayers during menstruation; this has nothing to do with their standing before God."

At the bottom of the social ladder stands the divorcée. The society treats her as a woman who has not proven herself as a wife, and she is blamed for breaking apart the family. Her chances of marrying a bachelor or a divorced man are slim, unless she marries someone much older than her or marries as a second wife.

# THE BEDOUIN HOME

Bedouin townships are now clogged with single-family houses. Often, one may find a Bedouin tent right next-door to a posh villa. The Bedouin find it difficult to part with the traditional tent. Ask a young Bedouin man, and he will often say that he misses the old days when the tent was the main living quarters—even if that was before his time.

Traditionally, the tent used to be divided into two parts, the northern part was for the men and their guests, and the women stayed in the southern part, away from the social activities in the tent. The guest will always approach the tent from the west, so as not to expose the women. When a man approaches the tents, he coughs loudly to signal that he is about to enter. The host will then come outside to greet the guest with *"ahlan wa'sahlan,"* a welcome that means, literally, "family and field"—that is, the desert and the home are yours. Once the guest enters the tent, everyone present rises, and the guest moves from one to another shaking hands.

A Bedouin man's virtue is often judged by his hospitality, which means keeping his tent open to any guest who shows up—whether invited or appearing unexpectedly. A Bedouin must always welcome a guest, regardless of financial means.

"Generous Bedouin hospitality is a direct result of life in the desert," explained Farhan abu-Shleibi, the energetic Bedouin entrepreneur whom we met at his tourist site in the northern Negev. "You can walk for days on end in the desert, and once you encounter the first tent encampment, you will be hosted, no matter what, regardless of who you are. This has turned out to be a permanent and mutual tradition among the people of the desert. Today you are my guest, tomorrow I will be yours."

The guest who enters the tent is considered a protégé of the host. It is the host's responsibility to guarantee the guest's safety, even if that guest is his enemy. The man is then seated, facing the north, to make sure that he will not have any eye contact with the women in their section to the south. The host sits in the northeastern corner of the tent to keep watch over his wife in the kitchen.

In the past, Bedouin hosts would feed and lodge a guest for as long as three days, no questions asked. By the middle of the fourth day, however, the host would dare ask the guest about the purpose of the visit. Nowadays, having been influenced by urban Western society, the host will sit and discuss business with his guest shortly after the first cup of coffee.

The guest is first offered a small cup with a very small amount of bitter coffee, followed by very sweet tea, re-enforced with herbs. The Bedouin interpret the small serving as a gesture of goodwill toward the guest: "We want you to stay longer, so we will serve coffee in small quantities. Had we filled up your cup, it would mean that we want you to drink up and leave."

*Bedouin hospitality*

The serving of the bitter coffee (*sada*) is considered a key element in the welcome ceremony. According to protocol, the host prepares the coffee before the eyes of his guest, grinding the coffee beans with a wooden pestle in a certain beat, occasionally pounding on the inside of the coffee jug. In the stillness of the desert, the pounding can be heard at a distance, a gesture of invitation to passing people to come and join the coffee ceremony.

Once the coffee is ready, the guest is supposed to drink whatever is in the cup in a gulp or two. If anything is left in the cup, he can spill it onto the sand floor, without insulting the host. He then returns the cup to the host. It is customary to carry out three rounds of coffee serving, the first for health, the second for love, and the last for future generations. It is considered disrespectful not to drink all three cups of coffee.

In the meantime, the wife, in the tent's kitchen, prepares very sweet tea, served with herbs found in the desert. The host continues serving tea until the guest makes it clear that he no longer wishes anything to drink. Those who are particularly keen on hospitality customs will once again serve bitter coffee as if to say: *Sweet tea was served to tell the guest that we are very happy to host him and that he gives our life an extra touch of sweetness. The bitter coffee indicates our sorrow that he must leave.*

The nutrition of the Bedouin depends largely on fruits, vegetables, and other gathered foods. A typical everyday dinner consists of rice, beans, vegetables, and pita bread, followed by a dessert such as baklava with coffee or tea. When a special occasion arises, such as a birth, marriage, a child reaching adulthood, or death, the Bedouin usually slaughter sheep for the main course in a festive meal.[3]

## TEMPTATIONS OF THE OUTSIDE WORLD

When the "outside world" penetrates the Bedouin home, it usually has adverse affects. One of the most serious health problems of Bedouin women is obesity, the result of leaving the traditional Bedouin diet in favor of Western junk food. A recent study conducted by Dr. Dov Tamir of Ben-Gurion University in Beersheba showed that an astounding sixty percent of Bedouin women are obese, with an additional twenty percent who are overweight. These figures are alarming. Illnesses that were once rare among the Bedouin are now on a steady upward trend. The rate of diabetes mellitus among the Bedouin is even higher than in the Jewish community, as are cardiac and vascular diseases, as well as common genetic diseases, which result from a high rate of marriages within the family.

The rate of skin cancer among the Bedouin population has caught up with the recent rise to around sixty percent among the general Israeli population. Dr. Tamir's conclusion is unequivocal: "We do not need more hospitals in the south; what we need is to educate the Bedouin population to lead a healthier life." This is the object of a new project sponsored by Ben-Gurion University medical faculty run by Dr. Tamir and his Bedouin assistant, Amal abu-Ghanem.

Dr. Tamir and his staff approached women in various locations and attempted to reverse the unhealthy effects of Western nutrition. Women were engaged in a five-month health-food training course—after they had received their husbands' permission, of course.

We met Tamir and abu-Ghanem at a ceremony marking the end of the "healthier life" course. The ceremony took place in a huge tent, where the dozens of Bedouin graduates of the course had found shelter from the scorching summer heat. Wearing a hat and sun-glasses, Dr. Tamir addressed the gathering. "I keep my hat and glasses to drive a point across," said Tamir. "Our conduct of life is not health-oriented. We must protect ourselves from the sun, and the Bedouin of the Negev are not excluded." He then turned to the Bedouin women and reprimanded their cooking habits: "You consume too much oil and cholesterol, and you are thus exposed to illnesses you had not known before. Our program is designed to save the next generation of Bedouin in the Negev. Rather than building more hospitals, we advise you to eat right, engage in more physical activities, and reduce the stress. The program works for the women, but through them it will affect their husbands and their children."

This is easier said than done. In a male-dominated society it is difficult for a woman to change her daily routine, and even more difficult to influence the men to change their eating habits and leisure time. Nevertheless, there are initial signs of change. Aside from lecturing them on healthy food, they have organized women's "walking groups." Amal has already noticed a slight change: Women increasingly use whole-wheat flour in their baking, while meat dishes give way to fish. Children who used to take chocolate and wafers to school now eat more fruits and vegetables.

## THE HAFLA

Nazha a-Saraya grabs a ball of dough, flips it rapidly from hand to hand, like a circus acrobat, until it becomes a large plate-like form, which she then throws over the rounded oven. Within seconds, the dough turns into delicious, hot pita bread that must be eaten fresh—a real celebration for any taste buds. The art of baking pitas is an absolute must for any Bedouin woman, the entry permit to the Bedouin kitchen.

Mama Nazha baked the pita outdoors, right next to a tent, set somewhere in the woods of Sartaneh, near Kibbutz Lahav in the Negev. Her son Omar erected the tent at the grazing area of his sheep as a sort of an outpost for the family's shepherds. Now that the grazing season was almost over, he decided to invite several dozen friends and family for a *hafla,* or a festive meal, out in the woods.

Omar a-Saraya, thirty-five, lives with his two wives and four children in the township of Hura, some twenty miles northeast of Beersheba. A sharp contrast exists between his home town and the tent in Sartaneh. Twenty years ago, Hura had been a conglomerate of tents and tin barracks, but in recent years, spacious modern houses, some even extravagant, have emerged from the desert sand—a vivid expression of the transformation sweeping the Bedouin society.

The town is still in a state of transition, with unpaved streets where children run freely—and dangerously—and no traffic signs. The Bedouin middle class has made the move from a nomadic into a semi-urban society. Omar, a supervisor at a textile factory in the Jewish town of Arad, is one of those who

*Omar a-Saraya with son*

have made the leap. "The state had forced the Bedouin to change their way of life, against their better judgment. They did it unwillingly. Fifty years ago the Bedouin of the Negev were happier people—even twenty years ago. People used to love each other; today things are different."

Omar misses the past. During the winter season, young members of the family take the family sheep to graze in the north. Omar often splits his time between work and his tent in the meadow, just as his father had done in the good old days. "When I was young I didn't like the sheep, but my late father liked them very much and saw them as part of our tradition."

Eventually Omar, too, learned to enjoy grazing the sheep. "Often when I come home from the factory I stay for only ten minutes, but then I come to the grazing area, make sure that everything runs okay, that the sheep have their food, water, and medication."

Sometimes he takes time away from his family and spends the night in the tent with his herds. He says that he prefers the shabby, worn-out tent to his multi-story villa, and the smell of the sheep to the cleanliness of the textile factory. "There is nothing better than this way of life," he said. "This is nature. The Bedouin is nature. I must not forget the tradition of my forefathers. When I am with the sheep, I feel that I am once again with my father. When I come here, I forget a lot of my troubles."

Every year, at the end of the grazing season, it is time for the seasonal *hafla*. A dirt road leads to the tent. The dogs greet us with loud barks. The women are busy heating up a fire in the back of the tent. Omar's fashionable jeep pulls by his tent. Omar gets out of the car, and approaches his mother. She reaches out her hand toward him; he then kisses the hand, and leans back turning his cheek toward the mother. She kisses him three times on his upper cheek, and then turns back to her pita. The mother is then busy baking the pitas over the home oven.

"We hold such an event at least once a year, sometimes even three or four times a year," said Omar. "This is our way to thank God for the good He has bestowed upon us during the year. This is also an opportunity to meet with old friends."

The sheep, which will soon be the main course of the meal, have already been slaughtered. The young men in the family have set up an improvised grill to fry the sheep. Grilling the sheep is their domain—the rice, the pitas, and the salads are part of the women's responsibility. There was no running water in the vicinity, so they needed a mobile container to bring water from the nearby kibbutz.

Shortly before the first guests arrived, Omar stood to the side to say the noon prayer, while the others proceeded with their work. "I like praying," he told us. "I feel better

*Women preparing meat for the hafla*

after praying. Sometimes, when I am late praying, I feel
that I have missed something, I feel the pressure, and that
is relieved only after the prayer."

One of the men now slaughters a goat. A girl shows
up with the head of a goat in her hand, handing it over
to Nazha. The women then cut the head into pieces and
throw it into a huge pot with boiling water, soon to become
steaming goat soup, a delicacy in the Bedouin kitchen.

In the meantime, more guests arrive. They remove their
shoes, put them aside in a row, and then sit on small carpets
spread beneath the trees. As each guest arrives, he greets all
present with a loud *"a-salam aleikum"* (peace be on you).
Everyone rises as the guest walks from one guest to another,
shaking hands before sitting and joining the company.

The younger men fill a hole in the ground with dried
twigs for the fire, an improvised stove soon to host large,
juicy parts of the just-slaughtered sheep.

*The men eating together*

Once the men have gathered for the meal, the youngest son goes to the cooking area and receives the food from the hands of his sisters. Then, along with his younger brothers, he serves the food. Because the Bedouin home lacks tables, chairs, and utensils, food is served on a giant pita placed on a carpet. Cushions are placed around the carpet for the men to sit and enjoy their meal. The host is traditionally expected to orchestrate the meal and conversation. Women do not enter the area during the meal. The women eat in a separate section of the tent or in a separate tent. Food is served in a similar setting, but it is always smaller and less luxurious than that of the males.

After they serve the meat, the young men return with pita breads in their hands, handing them to the guests. The pita is a basic component for any Bedouin meal. Rather than using a knife and a fork, the Bedouin tears the pita into small pieces, using them to collect chunks of meat, grab a ball of rice, or dip into the humus—the heavenly chickpea dish and the jewel in the crown of Middle Eastern food. Most important, the pita assures that one never—but never—leaves a Bedouin meal feeling hungry. The men eat quietly, everyone absorbed in the meal, and only whispers are heard.

Now that the pitas are all baked, mother Nazha makes tea, which will be served at the end of the meal. She puts a selection of herbs in a huge pot, puts it on a gas canister, and adds generous quantities of sugar. The Bedouin like their tea very sweet, a means of keeping themselves thirsty so that they keep drinking throughout the long, hot day.

During the grazing season, mother Nazha, too, goes out with the herds, just as she had done ever since she was twelve. She enjoys it just as much today. For her, going out with the sheep, means going back to the past. "Life used to be better, there were fewer problems. Even though there was not much food and money, people were satisfied with what they had. Of course, we thank God for the food and work he has given us, but look at the food—it is all full of chemicals. It used to taste so much better in the past. So are the girls. Today the girls have everything, but they do not make them anymore like they used to. Present-day girls could not have coped with daily challenges in the past."

## MARRIAGE

*"I am a Bedouin, an Arab, and a Muslim, but my values are foremost Bedouin. It is up to the man to decide whom his daughter will marry. This is mandatory. The honor of the family cannot be compromised."*
—SHEIKH SAMI ABU-FREH, the Imam of Rahat

As the night falls over the Bedouin town of Rahat, following a long and hot summer day, a cool desert breeze pampers the guests assembled for a wedding ceremony in a yard surrounded by makeshift tents. Loud wedding songs play over the public system, making it impossible to talk—but who feels like talking?

A group of about twenty women, dressed in colorfully embroidered, long black dresses, enter with colorful straw baskets full of sweets on their heads. They dance to the refrain, "Welcome the guests who have honored the bride and bridegroom." As they dance, the baskets do not move an inch—a special dancing skill. Surrounding and admiring the dancers are women and men, boys and girls, all dressed in their best attire. The concourse is lit by powerful lamps, which add to the festive atmosphere.

As the dancing picks up, young girls join the women, trying to show that they can do better. Young men stand by, watching the girls with hungry eyes. Gradually, the men

*The dancers enter*

form their own circles of *debka,* a popular Middle Eastern dance. They maintain complete separation between the men's and women's circles.

The wedding ceremony takes place only after the *qadi* (a religious judge) has authorized the marriage. Thus, by the time the festivities begin, they are already legally married. Even the details of the wedding ceremony are determined by the men in the family, with priority given to the bridegroom's father, who takes charge of arranging the ceremony "after consultations with the bride's father." The ceremony actually begins a few hours earlier with a luncheon at the house of the bridegroom's father. The bridegroom attends the lunch without the bride, while the bride's mother dresses up her daughter, and the two wait at home. In the evening, the two meet, and a member of the family drives the couple to the wedding ceremony.

*Marriage dance party*

Then comes the moment for which everyone has waited patiently. A car, decorated with colorful ribbons and flowers, arrives at the site. The young couple descends majestically from the car, the bridegroom dressed in elegant black slacks, white shirt, and a red tie, and the bride in a posh green dress, decorated with sparkling jewelry on a generous neckline, accentuating a tight waistline, with the bottom part of the dress opening like that of a ballerina. With a large green rose glued to her fresh hairdo, her arms are bare, which contrast sharply with the traditional appearance of the dancing women.

As the smiling bride approaches the guests with a bouquet of flowers in her hand, the master of ceremonies excitedly announces over the loudspeaker, "Please welcome the bride and the bridegroom!" Accompanied by cheers, the young couple walks on a white carpet between torches of sparkling fire as the women shower the bride with confetti. The groom's smile is broad and the bride's shy.

Then it is time for the bridal dance. Once again, the elder women, in traditional dress, join the dancing, while the master of ceremonies, speaking over the music in a loud voice, encourages the crowd to join the party. Normally, men and women dance separately on such occasions, but

*The bride and groom dance*

now the bridegroom dances with his beloved amid a group of dancing women, as though his special status excuses him from the rigid tradition of separation between men and women. The star of the evening is the bride's mother, her face covered entirely by colorful jewelry and chains of gold coins.

The wedding is an odd mix of generations, with some in traditional festive dress and others in modern dress; some women wear heavy makeup and others none at all; some cover their heads, and other show fancy hairdos. The wedding in Rahat seems to symbolize a meeting between the old and the new—desert tradition and the unavoidable challenges of modern, Western life.

In keeping with Bedouin tradition, the young couple retires to a tent after the wedding ceremony. It has been erected especially for them, and a number of horsemen remain beside the tent to "guard" the couple and make sure they are not disturbed. The next morning, the bridegroom's relatives enter the tent to make sure the young man has consummated the marriage, after which they escort the couple to the tent of the bridegroom's parents.

Nowadays, especially in the Bedouin townships, the process is much simpler; soon after the wedding ceremony, the young couple drives away for their honeymoon, preferably to a luxury hotel in the southern resort town of Eilat.

In the past, Bedouin girls were married off as soon as they reached puberty at the age of twelve or thirteen. Today, however, the marriage age for girls is sixteen, though the legal age is seventeen. Marriage at a younger age needs the special approval of a family court. Traditionally, a girl's freedom to choose a husband was quite limited. Usually, two families would agree on a match, even while the future bride and groom were still children. Occasionally, when two families were expecting children, the men of those families would agree that, if a boy and a girl were born, they would eventually marry each other. Such vows were considered irreversible, so that, even if one of the parents died in the meantime, the tribe's elders would see that the mutual promise was fulfilled.

The issue of marriage in the Bedouin society is so sensitive that, until very recently, Bedouin generally refrained from intertribal marriages. Each tribe considers itself the best, so it is difficult to volunteer a daughter to another, inferior tribe. "We take care of our daughters; once we marry them out of the tribe, other girls in the tribe will stay unmarried."

The notion of arranged marriages seems incomprehensible to the Western mind. Indeed, it is unacceptable even to many young Bedouin. Increasingly, young Bedouin choose their own partners, although, prior to marriage, they are not allowed to "date" in the Western style—at least not openly. Sheikh Sami abu-Freh of Rahat told us, "Usually we educate the daughter to follow the advice of her father, but it does happen that the daughter will choose a husband against his will. Religion does allow the girl to make her own choice, because the Qur'an rules that everyone is equal before God, but then there are the Bedouin customs that put obstacles on that choice. Thus, for example, according to our tradition, first choice is given to the cousin." According to tradition, he has the prerogative to "take the girl off the saddle, even on the day of her wedding to someone else." However, as time passes, traditions make way for more modern practices.

It is remarkable that so many relatively young and educated women and men (mostly men) still adhere to the old traditions, though not because they necessarily believe that are right, but out of reverence for those traditions. It is still common for the father of the boy to visit the girl's house and ask the consent of the girl's father for the marriage, as though the couple has no say in the matter.

Bedouin boys may get married as early as age fifteen, and girls may be married as soon as they reach puberty. Early marriage is considered a precautionary means of minimizing premarital sexual relations. "However," Sheikh Sami told us, "some things have changed with the times. Only twenty years ago, one could not have accepted marriage outside of the tribe; this was an absolute no-no. However, nowadays, with the world opening up, it is difficult for me as a father to insist on a preordained marriage. I shall not force my daughter into marriage. I may talk to her, advise her, try to influence her, but I shall not force her to wed a man against her will."

The most common form of marriage is endogamy, or marriage within the tribe. The logic for this is twofold; it reduces the chance that a girl will be involved romantically or sexually with partners who do not meet the tribe's standards, and it intends to reduce the number of unwed women in a tribe, since it is the duty of single men to marry the virgins of the tribe and, in some cases, widows and divorcées.

Nowadays, there are fewer Bedouin men than there are women, who accommodate this new reality in various ways. In a *badal* marriage, for example, two brothers simultaneously marry two sisters, or a brother and a sister marry a brother and a sister of another family, in effect avoiding the payment of a dowry, which may be as much as $7,000. Girls over thirty often compromise by marrying an older person rather than remaining at home with their parents. A groom's father, for example, may stipulate his consent for marriage in a deal that requires the bride's brother to marry his daughter, the bridegroom's brother.

Another solution is for a woman to marry a man much older than she is. Alternatively—and controversially, although Islam permits it—a man may marry as many as four wives. "A woman often prefers to marry an older guy to remaining a spinster in her father's house," said Qadi Dugan.

"According to our tradition, the first wife is chosen according to tradition. The second wife is chosen out of love," said Sheikh Sami. "This is why you will rarely find unmarried women over thirty."

Marriage is undoubtedly the ultimate expression of love between a man and a woman. In Bedouin culture, however, it is also a business transaction—more so certainly than in any Western society. A bride is considered the property of her parents. Thus, a wedding involves some market-like dealing. When the parents give her to be married, she actually leaves her family and joins her husband's family. Thus, the bride's family is compensated for this loss of "property," with the bridegroom's family paying the bride's family a dowry, bride price, also known as bride wealth. The bride price is determined by several factors:

- The bride's parents' "loss" of a daughter and their consent to send her off to a new life with a new family;
- Her family's "investment" in the girl through the years;
- The loss of a working hand in the parents' house;
- The bridegroom's family's payment for the belongings she brings from her parents' home;
- Payment in exchange for the bride's family's loss of her labor and fertility within her kin group.

By the end of 2007, the typical bride price stood at approximately $7,000 or the equivalent in property or other valuable assets, depending on the economic status of both families.

Incidentally, although the Bedouin live right next to large Jewish population centers, and although Bedouin young people often date Jewish girls, there are few mixed marriages because of the abundance of Bedouin women, because of tradition and family honor, and because Jews are also inclined against intermarriage with Arabs.

## Bedouin Women's Sexuality

Why do Bedouin men suppress their women? Why do they hide their sexuality behind thick dark veils instead of showing them off? Is it because, unlike Western society, they denigrate and downplay women's sexuality? According to researchers Al-Krenawi and Graham the opposite is true.[4]

Al-Krenawi and Graham found in their studies that the patriarchal Arab Muslim society considers the woman's sexuality to be very strong—so strong, in fact, that it can "disrupt the social order." They view women's sexuality as a family treasure to be kept in a safe place, away from alien, lustful eyes. As a result, from early adolescence, women accept the tribe's control over their general behavior, especially sexual behavior. A woman must observe "family honor." This is why a woman who deviates from accepted social norms is subject to heavy punishment, including excommunication from the tribe and even death, imposed by the family in defiance of modern state laws and at the risk of long years in jail.

The paradox of the matter is that, although sex plays a major role in Bedouin life, girls often reach their wedding night unprepared, not having been exposed to the basic facts of life. Only in recent years has the education ministry initiated sex education in the higher classes of high school, much later than girls' first menstrual period. Bedouin mothers are often too shy to discuss sex with their daughters, so they leave it for a sister-in-law or a married friend of the family.

Dr. Rania Abedelhadi, the first Bedouin woman to receive a doctor of medicine degree (whom we shall get to know better), has encountered many Bedouin women who had virtually no sex education. We asked her whether the mother prepares her daughter for menstruation. "No. Older sisters and cousins, but not mothers. The same applies to boys; they hear it from brothers and friends, but not from parents—unfortunately. My mother is involved with an NGO that deals with women's education in general and with sexual education in particular, although they do not call it sex education as such. The husband will not agree to send his wife to hear those things. They call it family or health education in general.

"Part of the program is lectures by doctors on women's issues such as contraception and breast cancer, and during those meetings they do ask sexual questions. I wrote an article about women's masturbation, but the NGO I worked with suggested that we do not publish it."

Islam bans sexual relations during the menstrual period. "The couple can sleep in the same bed, they can hug and kiss, but not have relations," Dr. Rania told us. "They can even have oral sex, but not intercourse. To the best of my knowledge, Islamic law does not say so explicitly, but this is the interpretation of it. She can give him oral sex, or vice versa. However, I do not know if Bedouin men do oral sex with women. I have never talked about it with women; it is much too delicate."

We asked if that meant she would not talk about it with a Bedouin woman unless she specifically asks whether it is all right for him to perform oral sex on her? Rania replied, "I have never discussed these issues, even with my closest friends and sisters—never."

One appalling practice that the Bedouin women in the Negev have been spared in recent years is female circumcision—the *tuhur,* which involves cutting the girl's clitoris to suppress her sexuality. Circumcised women are considered purer and thus more blessed than other women. This surgical act used to be quite common throughout the nomadic and rural societies of the Middle East and is still quite common among African Muslim societies, particularly those in Egypt and Sudan. Today, the practice is rare in Israel. Dr. Rania told us that she had never met women who had been circumcised. However, she did tell us that her sister, a social worker, conducted a study, and she found that as many as half of the female population above forty had been circumcised.

This finding has been supported by researchers Abed Asali and others.[5] Based on interviews with twenty-one Bedouin women, they concluded that the practice was common among several tribes. However, physical examination of thirty-seven young women from those tribes at a gynecological clinic revealed only small scars on the labia in each woman.

Dr. Rania explained that, even among those who had undergone the operation, rarely had it been total clitorectomy. "Usually they undergo partial cutting of the minor labia, or the major labia, but rarely the clitoris itself," she said. "When my sister conducted her survey, she met a ninety-one-year-old woman who told her, 'You look like someone who has not been circumcised; it's about time you do, and I am willing to do it for you.'"

## CHILDREN

Population growth rates among the Bedouin of the Negev is among the highest in the world. The annual increase stands at five percent; thus, by the year 2020, the anticipated number of Bedouin will be 320,000, twice their population in 2008. Here is a thought-provoking fact: According to a survey conducted in 2002 at Ben-Gurion University of the Negev, fifty-one percent of the Bedouin women do not practice birth control.[6] Among those who reported using birth control, the intrauterine device (IUD) was the most common method (thirty-eight percent). Only ten percent reported the use of oral contraceptives. Among those who did not use birth control, the most common reason offered was that they wished to get pregnant (forty-seven percent), while eleven percent mentioned that their husband objected to their use of birth control. Prof. Julie Cwikel noted that these data are true even among Bedouin women with higher education.

This is a classic case of the half-full cup. One should say this is real progress. Twenty to thirty years ago, Bedouin women rarely used any contraceptives. Moreover, compared to the Jewish Haredi community, this is a real breakthrough, since that community leaves birth control entirely to the "discretion of God." Nevertheless, half the Bedouin women continue to avoid the use of contraceptives.

It is important to interpret these data together with the data on the very high fertility rate among Bedouin women, noted Cwikel. Clearly, twenty to thirty years ago, very few used any birth control, she said—*but* their overall fertility rate was lower than today, because of many reasons: poorer nutrition and hygiene and a lower standard of living, as well as less access to the Israeli health care system.

Moreover, added Prof. Cwikel, a generation ago Bedouin women were much more likely to breastfeed for longer periods of time, thus using the natural system of child spacing, which is associated (at least in developing nations) with exclusive breastfeeding in the first year. Nowadays, Bedouin women are less likely to breastfeed for such a long period. Consequently, pregnancies are more frequent, and their overall fertility is greater.

Nevertheless, clearly the trend is toward birth control. In other words, here is another indication for a gradual departure from tradition, and yet another step toward women's liberation. The issue of multi-child families has become even more dramatic, owing to the fact that in recent years, even among the younger generation, the phenomena of bigamy and polygamy have increased, not decreased. In this respect, the Bedouin are different not only from their Jewish neighbors, but also from the vast majority of the Muslim population in Israel.

Women in polygamous families are less inclined (only thirty percent) to use contraceptives than those in single-wife families. Consequently, there is an average of 7.5 children per polygamous family, compared to five per normative family. This indicates that women in a polygamous family are either pressed to bear more children or feel the need to do so—in a sort of interfamily contest.

## BIGAMY AND POLYGAMY

*"Well, this is the way it works: In the beginning they are a happy young couple, very much in love. Then, gradually, the woman drives her husband crazy. So, he takes a second wife, hoping that she would sweeten his life. However, eventually she, too, drives her husband crazy, so that he gets a double dosage of it. When does he finally get his peace and quiet?—when the two women start quarreling with each other."*

—FARHAN ABU-SHLEIBI, a tourism
entrepreneur with one wife

Farhan's analysis was presented as a joke, but it reveals the Bedouin man's egocentrism; let the women suffer, as long as I have my pleasures—and my peace of mind. However, there is a punch line to Farhan's joke: "Eventually the two women grow old, they make peace with each other, and now both of them drive the husband crazy. And this is when the husband takes the third wife."

Many young—even well-educated—Bedouin take a second wife. They are available, so why not? There are no precise figures on this phenomenon, but according to a study carried out by the health ministry, some thirty-six percent of Bedouin women who seek medical assistance from the health services report that they are married to a man who has another wife. The study indicates a phenomenon that is becoming even more common through the years. Experts estimate the rate of multiple marriages among Bedouin men is between twenty-five and thirty percent. In other words, one in four Bedouin men is married to more than one wife.

In the past, many "second wives" were imported from the occupied territories, the West Bank and the Gaza Strip, for the simple reason that in those areas the dowry is much less expensive than in Israel proper. Others were brought from Jordan, where the majority of the population is Bedouin. This is no longer the case, as the territories are virtually closed off from Israel. Nevertheless, in recent years more and more young women agree to be the second, third, and even fourth wife in the family.

Rumor has it that Salman al-Husayel, a legendary sheikh in the Negev and long deceased, was married thirty-nine times. No one knows how many children he had, but, as far as anyone knows, his record still stands. Nevertheless, the practice of taking multiple wives is still quite common, despite the fact that it violates civil laws that ban bigamy and polygamy.

As strange as this practice seems from a Western perspective, and though it creates natural antagonism, Westerners should at least try to understand its background. The Bedouin place the roots for this practice in past times, when having more than one wife was considered not only customary but also a means of survival. Economic burdens created the need for many children to share the family workload. The economic logic was simple: the more women, the more children, the larger the family's workforce, the higher its standard of living.

"Bedouin like to have many children, particularly if the father is a sheikh or a rich man," Qadi Dugan al-Atawneh told us. "Why? Because in the old days, when tribal customs were the only customs and there was no central law and no military force, the more men one had in the tribe, the stronger the tribe was considered. This is called *izbeh* in Bedouin terminology."

Okay, so the Bedouin have lots of children, and lots of children are lots of fun—as long, of course, as one can provide them with adequate food, education... and love. But by now, Qadi Dugan, too, feels that this tradition has done more harm than good. "The more children one has, the fewer the means to provide them with all their needs. Many go to the fields rather than to school, thus lacking basic education. When they grow older and no longer enjoy grazing the herds, they seek easier and quicker money. Thus, the less educated youth tend to go astray, beginning with minor crimes, and may eventually engage in major criminal acts such as smuggling narcotics, breaking into the homes of well-to-do Jews, or extorting protection money from businesspeople in Beersheba."

Polygamy is not exclusive to the Bedouin. "If a man has two wives, and he loves one but not the other, and both bear him sons..." (Deuteronomy 21:15), says the Bible. King David had six wives and numerous concubines. His son, King Solomon, was much more efficient; he had 700 wives and 300 concubines. Polygamy was not banned in Judaism until Rabenu Gershom, around 1000 C.E. Not all Jews adhered to the ban, and it remained quite common, particularly among the Jews of Yemen.

The Mormons, too, practiced multiple marriages, but the Druze religion, which split from Islam, banned having more than one wife.

Polygamy among the Bedouin is the ultimate manifestation of the Islamic permission for such marriages. It is an expression of the inferior status of the Bedouin woman, who must be obedient. The woman has no right to choose her husband; she is not entitled to an inheritance; and in the case of divorce she usually does not get the children. Moreover, physical abuse of the woman is quite common in that society.

Sometimes the man will fictitiously divorce his first wife so that he will be legally registered with the state as married to only one wife. The divorcée is then considered a common-law wife. Both wives are entitled, of course, to allowances for the children, which, more often than not, are collected by the happy-go-lucky husband. Despite this widespread phenomenon, from 2000 to 2005 only 372 men reported marriages to a second wife to the interior ministry. Nevertheless, interior ministry officials estimate that some 216 children were born in 2005 alone to "second wives." Even population registry officials admit that official statistics do not quite reflect the scope of this phenomenon, because, through fictitious divorce and other means, the Bedouin try to carry out this practice indirectly to avoid violating the state law.

Even so, the "second wives" have proven to be a good economic investment. They are cheaper to acquire, and with each new child the family is entitled to receive a generous government allowance, which grows as the family expands. The state allocates children's allowances to the mothers, not to the fathers. Mothers are entitled to children's allowances, regardless of whether they are the first or the second wife in the family.

As of January 1, 2008, a family with five children could receive a monthly allowance of $330; ten children would add about $810 to the family's budget, twelve children $1,000, with each additional child worth $43. Thus, the children's allowance has contributed substantially to family budgets, which goes against the very interests of the state, as well as—as some would say—against the interests of the Bedouin people themselves. In other words, the state indirectly rewards bigamous and polygamous families, even though they conflict with the law.

Bigamy is a criminal offence in Israel. Article 176 of the Punitive Law of 1977 states that "a married man who weds another woman, and a married woman who weds another man, are subject to five years imprisonment." Nevertheless, the law has seldom been enforced, and only a few Bedouin men have ever been charged for violating the law. This conflict can also have tragic results. So long as they are not recognized as Israeli citizens, second wives who have been "imported" from the occupied territories or from other countries are not entitled to national health insurance. In some cases, terminally ill women have been refused free medical treatment because they were not insured.

So how has polygamy won out over the state law? A Bedouin man can wed a second wife according to *Sharia* (religious law). The marriage is performed by the *qadi* (a religious judge), yet the state population registry records the additional wife as common law only. Obtaining the approval of the religious court for such marriages is seldom

an obstacle. The couple need only show a marriage agreement signed by two Muslim men, and the court will approve
the marriage. The court does not require any clergy or state
officials to attend the marriage ceremony. As far as the court
is concerned, a couple that has signed such an agreement is
married in the eyes of the law.

Although the religious court is run by the state, usually
it does not report such marriages to the interior ministry,
simply because it is the court's prerogative to approve such
marriages. Once the *qadi* certifies the marriage, the state
has no choice but to honor the ruling.

How does one compromise between the Bedouin custom that allows multiple marriages and the state law that
bans it? It simply ignores the law. "I have no choice but
to grant a request to register a second wife, even though
it is considered illegal by the law of the state, the reason being that we must judge according to Muslim religious law," said Qadi al-Atawneh. Theoretically, the state
could sue the bigamous or the polygamous husband. In
the past it did, but no longer. "The state has given up,"
said al-Atawneh.

"The interior ministry is obliged to register marriages
performed by the *sharia* courts, even if they are unlawful
bigamist marriages," said Sabin Haddad, spokesperson for
the population administration at the ministry.

One may also circumvent the law by marrying a woman
and immediately divorcing her, whereas she continues to live
in the same house as a common-law spouse. Alternatively,
one may have a traditional marriage within the tribe, but
fail to register the additional wife in connection with the
man's identity card.

According to Beersheba Soroka Hospital officials, sometimes one of these women who are not Israeli citizens may show up at the maternity ward with the identity card of her husband's legitimate wife, so that the child will be recognized as an Israeli citizen and be eligible for children's allowance. The officials say jokingly that, among the Bedouin population of the Negev, some pregnancies seem to last only a couple of months, since some women report giving birth two or even three times a year.

How does the state cope with this open violation of its laws? It files complaints against bigamists and polygamists, but most of those reports gather dust in remote police stations. During the first decade of the twenty-first century, the ministry has filed about a hundred complaints a year, but few Bedouin men have been charged for having more than one wife.

This phenomenon is much less common among the rest of the Arab population in Israel. In recent years, it even decreased in neighboring Arab countries such as Egypt and the Gulf states.

In the end, bigamist and polygamist Bedouin men have managed to beat the system. However, the one area in which the state has taken action to reduce the number of "second wives" is to stem the flow of brides from the West Bank and the Gaza Strip. In the past, those women would begin a "gradual process" of naturalization immediately after marrying their Israeli husbands, though they were not Israeli citizens. However, the high court of justice ruled in 2005 that, because bigamous marriages are illegal, "second wives" would not be entitled to even begin the process of becoming Israeli citizens.

Multiple marriages introduce new elements of tensions among the members of a family—the women and their husband, the women themselves, and the children of the mothers. In most polygamous societies, no one challenges the status of the first wife as the "woman of the house." This is not true of Bedouin families, in which the second, usually younger wife can cost the first wife her status. The first wife feels neglected and unloved, while relations with her husband quickly deteriorate—again in contrast to the religious stipulation that the husband should treat all his wives equally.

Studies conducted by Prof. Alean Al-Krenawi, head of the social welfare department at Ben-Gurion University, showed that children in polygamous families tend to suffer more from psychological problems than do those in monogamous families. Such children tend to drop out of school and are more likely to engage in delinquent behavior. Similarly, women in polygamous families suffer from low self-esteem and tend to suffer from depression. "The children of one wife tend to show hostility toward the children of the other wives," said Al-Krenawi. "They compete with each other for the love of the father and for his financial support. Conflicts among the women influence their respective children."

Why are polygamy and bigamy so popular among Bedouin men? Perhaps the first wife does not meet the accepted standards; she may be barren or give birth only to girls. She may suffer from mental illnesses, or perhaps she does not satisfy her husband in bed. Tribal traditions dictate marriages; if there are not enough men in the tribe, they take more than one wife. This, incidentally, has also been the justification for multiple marriages in other countries that have banned bigamy, including Chechnya, where the balance between men and women has been upset because of the many men who have fallen in battle. Multiple wives are also considered a sign of wealth and high social status. Many men are convinced that having more than one wife is a token of one's manhood. Moreover, multiple wives in a family are considered an economic asset and cheap labor.

Another reason for polygamy in modern times is the fact that many young men are forced to marry very young, in a prearranged marriage, usually inside the family. Once the man grows older and becomes economically independent, he feels that he can marry a second wife, this time of his own choice. Marrying a second wife is much easier than getting a divorce and confronting the family of the first wife. The roots for this custom can be found in the Qur'an:

> And if you have reason to fear that you might not act equitably towards orphans, then marry from among [other] women such as are lawful to you, [even] two, or three, or four: but if you have reason to fear that you might not be able to treat them with equal fairness, then [only] one—or [from among] those whom you rightfully possess. This will make it more likely that you will not deviate from the right course. (Sura 4: a-Nisa [the Women], verse 3)

What a wonderful world for the Bedouin man! Divine permission to enjoy the love of as many as four women simultaneously. However, the Qur'an itself realized that polygamy is a risky business. "Ye are never able to be fair and just as between women, even if it is your ardent desire" (ibid., verse 129).

Contemporary leading Islamic clerics, such as Sheikh Yusef Kradawi of Egypt, have issued many *fatwas* (legal opinions) allowing and supporting polygamy. In these *fatwas*, Sheikh Kradawi explains, the "equality" refers to the material side of the relationship—housing, clothing, food, and so on. In addition, the husband must divide his nights equally between his wives. As for the affairs of the heart, according to him, this matter cannot be controlled by anyone.

"There is no society without polygamy. Westerners who condemn and reject polygamy are doing it themselves. The difference between their polygamy and our polygamy is that theirs is immoral and inhuman. The man [in the West] sleeps with more than one woman, and if [the second woman] gets pregnant, he denies responsibility for the child and does not support the woman financially. It is nothing more than lust," wrote Kradawi.

Sheikh Kradawi, as well as a popular Saudi preacher, Dr. Tarek Swidan, the head of the European council of Fatwa, and many other scholars consider polygamy a natural and sacred institution that benefits society and guards against immorality.

The European council of Fatwa states, "A woman's inability to have children is another argument for polygamy by Islamic leaders. In Islam, if a man wishes children, he does not have to divorce his first, barren wife. He can take a second wife and still take care of the first."

Here is an indication of the radicalization process undergone by present-day Islam. Contrary to present-day preachers such as Kradawi and Swidan, religious leaders in the past did have their reservations regarding this practice. Such was the Mufti Muhammad Abdu, one of the most important Muslim thinkers in the nineteenth century. Abdu suggested that the Qur'an had actually meant to allow marriage to additional women only in extreme cases, such as with barren women. He warned that marriage to more than one woman is usually a reason for jealousy among the women and their children, because the husband cannot refrain from preferring one woman to another. Consequently, rela-

*Farhan abu-Shleibi with Ruth*

tions within the family sour and this can affect negatively not only the family but the entire society. Thus, he said, the Qur'an aims to limit bigamy and polygamy as much as possible, rather than allow it.[7]

As early as 1899, Kasem Amin, an Egyptian intellectual, argued in his book *Liberation of Women* that polygamy should be prohibited as an ill-practiced and wrongful tradition.

Farhan abu-Shleibi, forty, a young leader who emerged in the Negev outside the traditional tribal framework, agrees with Abdu. "I have one wife, and there shall be no other," said Farhan. "I believe in neither polygamy nor bigamy." Not only for the sake of healthy marital relations, but also for the sake of the children. "I am strongly convinced that the more educated and advanced children in our society are those who were born in a single-wife family." Farhan even keeps distance from polygamous husbands, "lest I be infected, too."

"One chooses the first wife out of tradition, so that she does not remain single, but the second wife is chosen out of love," Sheikh Sami abu-Freh of Rahat told us. "That is why there are very few girls who remain unmarried after thirty. The first wife objects, but she cannot prevent it. Only if there is full equality can one marry four wives."

"Marrying another wife is a matter of privilege, not duty," continued Sheikh Sami. "If you can grant all your wives full quality it is okay. However, if you have the slightest doubt that you will not be able to treat them equally in the bedroom, in food, in housing, and with the children, then you must not leave your first wife. You should never forget to return to the bed of your first wife. This is very difficult for the man, although it is not mandatory to exercise sexual relations every night. After all, sexual relations are a function of mutual feelings, emotions, and desires." Here again, a rather liberal interpretation of "equality."

Can a man love all his wives equally? Sheikh Sami did not hesitate for a moment. He knew the right answer: "This is a matter of the heart, between the man and himself." In other words, *no;* there is no full equality. Parents can love all their children equally. A man cannot love *all* his wives.

Having more than one wife, of course, changes the balance between men and women, creating a situation in which some men will be left without women. This takes us back to previous times and to the old tradition that explains and even justifies everything. Historically, religious permission to marry more than wife was adopted by Bedouin precisely because of the opposite phenomenon: a lack of young men. "In the old times," explained Farhan abu-Shleibi, "many men used to be killed in battle; thus, the women were shared among the men who were left in the tribe."

Researchers Julie Cwikel and Nurit Barak of Ben-Gurion University revealed some interesting facts in their study about bigamous and polygamous families.[8] Their breakdown of the female population among the Bedouin of the Negev showed that some sixty percent are first wives, thirty-one percent are second wives, and a only small percentage are third or fourth wives. Of the first wives who agreed to speak about their status in the family, about forty percent reported that their status had indeed worsened after their husband took a second wife; surprisingly, however, twenty-five percent reported that their status had improved. Almost half of the respondents (48.5 percent) were born to polygamous families, which increased the chances that they themselves would become part of a polygamous family. More than half (59.2 percent) of the women who married into polygamous families came from polygamous families, compared to 40.8 percent from monogamous families.

Na'ama al-Badur, director of the welfare department at the Tel-Sheva township, told us that, contrary to common belief, even young and educated men are likely to marry more then wife. "The phenomenon is spreading rather than disappearing."[9]

The government can do very little to curb this phenomenon, which is often described as a deliberate attempt by Arabs to tip the demographic scale in the Negev. Prof. Arnon Sofer of Haifa University, the most vocal critic of this so-called Bedouin expansionism, says that the natural growth among the Bedouin in the Negev from 2003 to 2007 has reached more than five percent, meaning that the population should double every twelve to fifteen years.[10]

Studies by Prof. Cwikel of Ben-Gurion University showed that women in polygamous marriages have a significantly higher fertility rate than women in monogamous marriages, because their social status in the family is increased by the number of children they bear, especially male children.

Unless felony is proven, multi-children Arab families are entitled to the same financial benefits that Jewish families receive. Although the government has tried to introduce new legislation to end the practice, they have had little success so far. In 2008, the government again revealed a plan to cope with this phenomenon. Yitzhak Herzog, minister of welfare, offered a provocative statement and instructed his ministry to take action: "Multiple marriages among the Bedouin amount to an epidemic."[11] Rather than sanctioning men with more than one wife, however, the ministry took the easy way out and launched an information campaign, including lectures at Bedouin high schools that encourage Bedouin women to go out to study and work.

"This phenomenon requires sensitive treatment, not a patronizing and preaching approach," said Herzog. The goal of the program was to raise Bedouin awareness of the negative aspects of polygamy, to recruit educators and clergymen for the campaign against polygamy. One of the goals of that new campaign is to instruct social workers on how to cope with problems in polygamous families.

In some cases, women protest against the husband's decision to marry a second wife. This turns into a power struggle in the family. If the wife is not strong enough, the husband can easily divorce her according to *sharia*, or Muslim religious law, granting the divorced woman few if any rights, often depriving the woman of her children, since the children stay with the father according to *sharia*. Thus, a woman's choice is often between divorce and compliance with her new status.

"They come to us crying," said Na'ama al-Badur, head of the welfare department at the Tel-Sheva municipality. "They ask why he had done it to them; they feel humiliated, having to live in the same house with a new wife or next door to her. Yet they would rather stay married, even as a second wife, because this has more important status than a divorced woman in the Bedouin society."[12]

The one positive aspect in this state of affairs is the feeling that the enlarged family provides mutual responsibility. Although the first wife lives in a sort of family "prison," she generally knows that her livelihood is guaranteed. Even if her husband divorces her, she will not be thrown out to the street. She will be taken back by her parents or other relatives.

## NA'AMA AND OMAR

Bigamy and polygamy are not limited to the older generation. In recent years, they have become quite popular also among younger men, even among the Bedouin middle class. Omar a-Saraya, from the village of Hura, was modest: "For the time being, two wives will do," he told us, half-jokingly. Omar is relatively young, educated, and earning a decent living as a supervisor at a nearby textile factory. He is typical of the younger generation, so one might expect him to oppose such traditional practices, or at least feel apologetic

*Omar a-Saraya with Na'ama and children*

toward them. Omar, however, feels quite satisfied with his choice to make love to two women and raise two sub-families within a single larger family.

Omar's first wife, Amina, is twenty-four and the mother of his three daughters, Manar, Mira, and Reem. Then Omar married Na'ama, who is a thirty-one-year-old educated divorcée. Na'ama Dabsa and Omar a-Saraya met by chance three years earlier, which is uncommon among the Bedouin, whose marriages are usually prearranged. Na'ama had been sitting with her mother at the cancer ward in the Beersheba Hospital, where her mother was to receive chemotherapy. As they sat and waited, the mother and daughter conversed with another patient, a Jewish woman who had emigrated from Russia. Naturally, the conversation revolved around health problems. Na'ama told the woman about a traditional Bedouin medication and suggested it might help with her illness. She jotted down her "prescription" in Arabic, along with her name and phone number.

The next morning, the Russian woman's husband took the paper to work and showed it to his Bedouin friend Omar a-Saraya. He asked Omar how he should go about obtaining the herbal medication. Omar had no idea, so he picked up the phone and called Na'ama for instructions. One call led to another, and eventually they met. It was love at first sight, they said. Omar chose Na'ama for his wife—his second wife.

"This is indeed an exceptional case," conceded Na'ama. "Usually a woman cannot meet with a man before the wedding. If it does happen, reactions from the girl's family can become quite unpleasant; at times they may even end up with murder."

Murder? Is that really so, or has Na'ama exaggerated a bit? In fact, in the Bedouin society—and to some extent Arab society in general—improper conduct by a female member of the family (and it may even be just suspicion of illegal conduct) still often results in the murder of that woman by a close relative, sometimes even the father or a brother.

Na'ama smiled apologetically, as if she meant to say: *Listen, people, I am just as shocked by these customs as you are, but what can I do?* However, when we asked her what she thought about this custom, she recited the old mantra: "We have our tradition that we must observe. Today, when I see how the Jewish girls behave, without any rules, do you think this open relationship between men and women is okay? Girls are sometimes so promiscuous that they might get pregnant without even knowing who the father is. This is why tradition is important, and sexual relations between a man and a woman can be held only after an official wedding. I do go to town, exposed to Western

*Na'ama in the kitchen*

society, but at the same time I do not forget my tradition. I must adopt the good things of the Western world, but we should not forget our culture and tradition, which we must protect."

*What about matters such as murder for family honor?* "Of course I oppose that, but such murders can be averted if the girl is prepared properly for the danger. Most murdered girls were between the ages of fifteen and eighteen. This is a dangerous age; she must be warned. The parents must prepare them for the challenges and how to behave, so that no one in the family doubts her behavior and morality."

Had Na'ama not been a divorcée, she conceded, she would not have married a man who was already married, but as a divorcée her stock in the match-making market were quite low—even though she was a virgin. "My first marriage was unfortunate," she told us, lowering her voice as if revealing a family secret. "We were young, in our early twenties. There was nothing between us, not even sexual relations. I remained a virgin. So my first marriage had come to an end. My father was dying; he wanted me to marry before he died, so I married Omar as his second wife. A woman who has never been married before is reluctant to marry a man with another woman, but a divorcée has very little choice; it's very difficult for her to find an available man."

Na'ama was born in Lagiya, Hura's neighboring Bedouin township. Had it not been for family pressures, she would have continued to immerse herself in education, as she had from early youth. "At first, my parents objected to my studies, because they did not want me out of the home. However, eventually they supported me. Actually, they had no choice. I simply explained to them that this is my choice and they will not change it."

Na'ama is the opposite of Amina, Omar's first wife. Na'ama is talkative, assertive, and exceptionally open for a Bedouin woman. When she married, Na'ama was about to complete her bachelor studies in Middle East history at Ben-Gurion University and was already working as a teacher. She was hardly the woman one would expect to become a number two wife, but she wanted to remarry. Her only other choice, most likely, was to end up an old spinster. She needed to compromise, as did Omar. He knew it would be best to allow his new wife extra time for her work and studies.

After half a year of marriage with Omar, she received her B.A. and continued to study for her Master's in education. "Teaching is the best job for Bedouin women. The teacher leaves and returns home at a specific time. The husband always knows his wife's whereabouts; there are no surprises. She is back in the early afternoon to care for the children."

In fact, however, it is not that simple. Like career women anywhere in the world, Na'ama leaves her child in the morning with a nanny (*not* Omar's other wife) and finds time only in the late evening hours for household work.

None of Na'ama's three sisters studied at the university. Unlike Na'ama, they did not dare to confront their parents, who objected to their daughters studying. As a result, Na'ama's sisters were married early. The choice for Bedouin women is very often between marriage and studies. Many girls choose studies because they are determined not be satisfied with a minor role in the household. On the other hand, many go out to study for the simple reason that they have not found husbands.

"Some men refuse to marry an educated woman," said Omar. "Frankly," he added, "I do not quite understand it. There is more common language with a woman who understands something in life. I thought I needed a woman who would help in life, also economically. It is easier to get along on a daily basis."

Omar did not plan to have two wives; it just happened that way. In fact, when he first married, he opposed bigamy. Then, after three years of marriage, he wanted another wife, "I don't know why. Things happen; some men do not get married for years and then eventually have three wives."

Although Na'ama compromised her status as the second wife, she was determined not to make any compromises regarding her studies. After her first child Zeid was born, Na'ama went out to study and received a teacher's certificate. She received a pleasant surprise. Many Bedouin men are not keen on having an educated woman in the house. Traditionally, the man has been considered the family wage earner, and the woman's place was in the field, the kitchen, and the bed. If a man was unable to fulfill the needs of his family, he was not considered a real man. Omar, however, not only encouraged his wife to study, but he also jokes that he would like to retire early and have his second wife bring in the dough. "If my wife was the main wage earner, I would respect her, not only because of the money, but also because of her personality," said Omar, who wears the attire of a progressive and liberal man. "I am waiting for her to become a school principal, so that she will bring the money and I will not need to work."

When asked what he thought about the progress of Bedouin women, Omar said, "I have no problem with that, as long as she does not deviate from the straight Bedouin way. This is not simple. I want her to study and to work, but if she goes astray, if we give up our honor and tradition, then it's not worth it." Na'ama agreed: "We have a heritage of which we are proud. Without it, we are worthless."

Omar, like other husbands in bigamous families, defends his right to have more than one wife on religious and traditional grounds. He rejects the notion that it is simply a matter of male ego. He claims just the opposite, that it is actually an act of altruism. Because of the shortage of men with good incomes, many girls would remain unmarried without the opportunity to become second wives. Bigamous and polygamous husbands also argue that they respect the main stipulation of Prophet Muhammad, who allowed polygamy if the husband is financially able to care for additional wives and is able to share his attention among the wives equally and justly.

For the record, Omar sees no problem whatsoever with having more than one wife, and there is no reason, he said, why his wives should have any problem with it. "They must be friends, and I am doing my utmost to make them friends, although I realize that there will always be tension, because every woman wants to have the man for her own."

The family lives in a three-story house on the edge of the village, overlooking a valley and surrounded by yellow desert hills as far as the eye can see. Although Omar shares a house with his brother and his family, there is plenty of room. The third floor is still closed off, waiting for the family to expand. "The house can easily accommodate three families for the rest of our lives." He said.

According to religious law, Omar alternates his nights between the two women. Na'ama lives in a small house next to the big family house. Thus he makes a point of sharing the nights, "one night here, and one night there, that's the way it is with our religion; that's obligatory, even if I am tired."

Omar was asked with whom he communicates best: "This is a secret between me and myself. I will also not tell you whom I love more."

Na'ama, who listened carefully to our conversation with Omar, had been polite enough not to interrupt. When she heard him say this, however, she exclaimed, "This is the opportunity to find out! Yes, ask him whom he loves more." Omar would not give in. According to religious law, he needed to love them both equally.

Asked how a woman feels about sharing a man with another woman, Na'ama said, "Yes, it's difficult, really difficult. Every woman wants her husband to be with her all the time; that's natural. Yes, sometimes I am sad that he is not with me—just like no man would like to share his wife with another man."

Suddenly, Omar showed greater understanding for the suffering of his wives. "If I had to share my wife with another man, I would be burning inside, I could not stand it, just like they feel." Now it was Na'ama's turn to show greater openness: "Well, it is not the same; we wives cope with it better. We understand that we need to compromise in order to go on with life."

"No cola in the house?" Omar roared as he entered Na'ama's kitchen. Na'ama ignored him, and continued to cook lunch. It is a modern kitchen, equipped with the latest refrigerator, a microwave oven, and a gas heater. Na'ama wore a knitted head scarf.

The three girls (Amina's three girls) were watching a Latin American soap opera on television. In appearance, it was a typical middle-class Western home, even as it sat on the edge of a Bedouin town in the middle of the desert.

What is for lunch? Fried potatoes, *labaneh* (yogurt cheese), fresh salad, and, of course, pita bread. No forks and knives. The children helped themselves with the pita. The young girls wore black headscarfs and black robes, their lips accentuated with a pink lipstick, a mixture of tradition and modernity, East and West, modesty and feminine touches.

After the meal, Na'ama carefully washed the dishes, trying to conserve water. Not long ago, running water was rare; one had to carry water by donkey from a nearby well or from an official water supply point.

Only on special occasions do both sides of the family meet for family meals. Since the two wives live separately, they each attend to their own area and children. Each has her own kitchen. They talk to each other, but there is no real cooperation. They do not even shop together, which, in any case, is generally left to the husband.

Omar and Na'ama can agree on one thing: their children would not have more than one partner in life. "My son will only have one wife. I hope this problem of bigamy and polygamy will be resolved soon, but I know it will probably take another fifty years, when the present generation exists no more. It will take quite some time, because there are roots of thousands of years that need to be uprooted," said Na'ama.

If Na'ama were to have a daughter, would she be different from her mother or the same? "I am sure that, in many respects, she will be luckier. No one will oppose her studying and choosing a profession, and she will be able to say what she wants. But, in order for that to happen, I need first to educate her properly—most important are the social norms. If she goes out to study, and if she does not have self-respect and is not respected by others, then there is no point in life."

"I believe that my daughter will not be a second wife," conceded Omar.

Omar is the older brother, which makes him responsible for the entire family. No major family decisions take place without consulting him first. Moreover, this is true of all brothers, even those who are married. Since the death of Omar's father several years earlier, this applies also to his mother. She does not need to obey her son blindly, but she will give his advice extra weight and usually do what he says.

In most families, bigamy and polygamy do little good for the children. These practices create jealousy among children of different wives, and the more children there are in the family, the less parental guidance there is. The children (especially the girls) take part in the household chores from an early age, often skipping school and missing out on an advanced education. Many girls marry early and, in turn, give birth early, adding to the population growth.

Omar's first wife Amina was absent when we visited. She refused to talk to us, her silence revealing as much as Na'ama's candid conversation. Amina was present in the house, but avoided the curious strangers. "She is shy," said Omar, but perhaps he was not too keen to show her. Unlike Na'ama, she did not receive an education, and Omar wanted to show the family's progressiveness. As a result, we never heard her side of what it is like to live with Omar and Na'ama.

Perhaps this widespread practice of multiple wives is the result of unsatisfactory marriages and the fact that parents force couples to marry early. Once a man has matured and become more economically independent, he may decide he can afford a second wife, which is more convenient than separating from his first wife and facing an unpleasant confrontation with the family of his first wife.

We asked Qadi Dugan why women are not allowed to marry more than one husband, since religion considers men and women equal. He explained that this is simply because the identity of the father would not be known in such cases. "The Bedouin like to make many children. When the first wife tires out the second comes, and this may be the case for up to four wives."

Qadi Dugan's late father, Sheikh Mousa al-Atawneh, had four wives, even though he was a member of the progressive socialist Mapam Party. As the ruling sheikh of the tribe, he took full advantage of the Bedouin custom of marrying a woman from each of the most important families in the tribe. "He treated all four wives equally. All four women lived in the same house. When they were young, it was quite difficult; but now that father is no longer alive, they get along just fine in their old days. After all, it is quite difficult for them to remarry."

Qadi Dugan is the father of two boys and five girls. He divorced his first wife in 1991 and is happily remarried. He said that he would not take a second wife. Even though he often ratifies bigamous and polygamous marriages, and despite the precedence set by his father, he feels that having more than one wife is out of the question.

Westerners have long been fascinated by the phenomenon of polygamy. The mysterious, enticing harems of ancient Arabian tales and the beautiful concubines and wily eunuchs of *The Thief of Baghdad* have given polygamy an exotic Eastern flavor for those who see the "Orient" as no more than an exciting and distant fairy tale. Although polygamy is associated with tales of the distant past, it is still very much alive. It is still practiced in the majority of Islamic countries, where it is permitted by law. During the twentieth century, it reached European and American shores with the waves of immigration from Islamic countries. People from Mali, Egypt, Mauritania, Pakistan, and other countries who immigrate to Europe often arrive with their extended families, which may include two, three, and even four wives and their offspring. Although European countries ban this practice, they turn a blind eye to its existence, much as Israeli authorities have done.

Egyptian feminists Huda Sharawi and Nawal Sa'adawi have demanded that polygamy be abolished as a backward practice that disgraces and enslaves women. Nevertheless, Tunisia is the only Arab country that has completely banned all forms of polygamy. Other countries, such as Morocco and Malaysia, which boast of a harsh policy toward polygamists, still hesitate to ban polygamy altogether and go against the powerful Islamist lobby. Following the latest decision of the Moroccan parliament, polygamous marriages are permitted only in exceptional cases, and only then with the approval of the first wife. A similar condition exists in Libya.

This situation is much worse in Egypt, which in 1985 amended progressive legislation of the late President Anwar Sadat, the so-called Jihan law of 1979 (named after his wife), which demanded that a husband produce written consent from his first wife before he marries another. Now the husband needs only to notify his first wife by mail.

In 2003, Malaysia, which previously had made it difficult for a man to marry more than one woman, eased that law in the state of Perlis, which is now known as a "polygamous paradise."

In Saudi Arabia, Jordan, Kuwait, Afghanistan, and the Palestinian Authority, a husband can bring an additional wife into the home without even discussing the matter with his first spouse.

As a part of life in Muslim countries, the situation of multiple wives with one man becomes fodder for television and movies. A few years ago, an Egyptian series, *Al-Hajj Mutawali,* told the story of a man with four wives. It was aired during the month of Ramadan and instantly became a hot topic in the press. *Another Lady,* a similar Iranian series, enraged a group of Iranian women activists, who denounced the government for trampling women's rights. Sometimes the husband in such shows is presented as a comedic figure, trapped between two furious women, as in the Afghani show *The Two Wives,* a big hit in the 1970s.[13]

## HONOR KILLING

Although the "Islamic Movement" has spread among the Bedouin, just as it has among the Arab population of Israel and the Arab world in general, there is one case in which religion allows for the tribal law: honor killing. This is generally a punitive murder, committed by male family members against a female of the family whom that family and/or the wider community believe has brought dishonor to the family.

Killing women for the sake of "family honor" remains one of the most acute problems for Bedouin women. If a woman does not obey the rules, she can face capital punishment by the family. It is up to the men in the family, usually the father or brothers, to determine which rules are applicable and how to interpret them.

Situations that violate "family honor" include prostitution, premarital sexual relations, adultery, refusing an arranged marriage, seeking a divorce (even from an abusive husband), and rape. Yes, the rape victim is often considered just as guilty as the rapist is. Such killings arise from the perception that, regardless of the situation, a woman bears the responsibility for dishonoring the family. Even when she is the victim of a rape crime, it is assumed that she provoked the crime through her behavior. Several men we interviewed stated with certainty, "A girl who has sex before marriage has no right to live."

Some testimonials were horrific. "I have daughters in high school, and I am quite worried," Ali a-Saraya told us. "It happened in the past that girls who flirted with boys were punished by death—regardless of the price, and even if the killer went to prison for twenty years. After all, he is not the real killer; neither is his family. It is not the family that kills; rather, the family executes the verdict of the society. If the honor of my daughter is violated, I have no choice but to kill the violator. I use a knife for work at home and to slaughter the sheep. If I need to use it to protect my daughter, this is better than an Uzi submachine gun."

Indeed, a key to understanding Middle Eastern thinking and politics is *honor*. A violation of one's honor is sometimes considered more harmful than bodily or financial harm.

A Bedouin who feels that his *ard* (land) or *ard* (a woman's honor, pronounced slightly differently, with the "a" deeper in the throat) has been violated is unlikely to forgive and more likely to seek revenge. He may go so far as executing the violator, despite the clear religious ban on murder. In the desert, the rule of the desert supersedes the rule of Islam.

Sheikh Sami abu-Freh, the Imam of the Bedouin township of Rahat, wrote in his Master's degree thesis that, although blood vengeance is considered a legitimate traditional practice, it is absolutely contrary to religious edicts. "Religion bans murder, even if the wife is adulterous," said abu-Freh. "However, there is a clash here between the religious edict and the tribal law, and in this case, the tribal law often supercedes religious taboos. Bedouin customs sometimes distort the religious law to serve the man's interests." So, here is where religion clashes with the tribe, where the Holy Qur'an clashes with the rule of the desert. So, what to do? Education is the key. The problem with religion—all religions—is that people feel free to make their own interpretations; it is up to the moderate elements of a society to reconcile religious law with tribal tradition. This is the mission that abu-Freh has assumed. "I have found myself in the midst of Islam, real Islam, not the distorted Islam you see on television. There is only one Islam, the real one, which we received from the Prophet Muhammad (peace be upon him). There is a moderate Islam and extremist Islam. There is only one Islam, which unfortunately everyone twists according to one's interests, and this is very sad."

What does Islamic law say about honor killing? Qadi Dugan told us, "According to Islamic law, if a married woman commits adultery, she must be executed, provided there is evidence of four witnesses that she had indeed betrayed her husband. However, since it is highly unlikely to have four witnesses to an act of adultery, the law in effect rules out capital punishment. Unfortunately, once again, tradition is stronger than religion. If a man is convinced that his wife has slept with another man, he will have no difficulty whatsoever to present the four witnesses, even if none of them had actually seen her doing it."

Ali a-Saraya puts the blame on the media, which he believes have a strong negative affect on Bedouin boys and girls, legitimizing what should not take place. "The other night I watched a TV program about eight couples, where each betrays the other. I saw a sixteen-year old girl going to bed with her boyfriend, warning him to take it easy with her because she was still a virgin. Her boyfriend vomited. How disgusting. When my children see this, they get a wrong example. It is no good for my daughter to watch this."

Studies show that Bedouin women are indeed highly exposed to violence.[14] According to a study at Ben-Gurion University, some forty-eight percent of the women interviewed reported that they had been exposed to violence, while forty-five percent had been exposed to repeated bouts of violence, often victims of a family member.

## "Hardly a Day Passes that I Don't Get Beaten"

Many married Bedouin women live as captives. There are no physical bars or chains, but they are virtual slaves to their husbands. They must obey their orders, cannot go anywhere without their permission, and cannot study without their consent. Such restrictions are supposed to protect the woman's honor. Bedouin men rely on religion to justify the limitations they impose on women. Religion forbids a woman to go out on her own, men say; she should not be approached by other men; she must always be escorted by a member of the family, even when shopping or going to a clinic. She is certainly not allowed to drive. Moreover, 'once she is finished, she must return home without delay. Anyone unwilling to follow such rules, the conservative Bedouin say, is not a real Bedouin. This is essentially a sentence to a life of captivity, sometimes with hard labor.

Na'ima, twenty-one, is this kind of "slave." She has been married for five years and, by her husband's orders, must remain in the home and take care of her husband and children. We met her clandestinely in the Bedouin township of Rahat. Jalila, an activist Bedouin woman, brought her along to our meeting. Na'ima had told her husband she was going to the doctor. Her virtual chains are always present, even when she is far from home among the abu-Kaf tribe, and even when her husband is away from the tribe. Family members keep a watchful eye on Na'ima, always spying on her.

Na'ima was schooled only up to the sixth grade at the desert elementary school. By order of her father, she was removed from the school. "They were afraid that I would elope with someone—and I was only twelve years old."

When she was sixteen, she was forced to marry her husband, a family relative. "'This is your cousin,' they told me. 'Marry him and that's it.' At sixteen, I knew nothing. I had no idea how children were brought to the world."

Two years later, she had her first child. Another year passed, and she had her second child. When she took her children to the mother-and-child clinic, she could not explain what she needed, because the Jewish nurse could not speak Arabic, and she knew very little Hebrew. It was the first time she felt the urge to study, at least study some Hebrew, so that she could cope more easily with everyday life. However, there was no one with whom she could discuss it. Her husband, too, had received only a basic education. He completed eight years of school, and worked at a metal factory. Life has been a painful routine ever since. "I work all day in the house, wash and clean like an ox, like a donkey. I attend to the sheep, and I better do it right. If my husband sees even one stalk of straw under one of the sheep, he pulls out the whip and whips me. He is very jealous of me. He may beat me even for just watching a couple kissing on TV. Hardly a day passes that I don't get beaten."

Na'ima is all alone and cannot seek help even from her own family. Her father, too, who has five wives, shares the view that the woman has nothing to look for outside her home. He used to say that he knew women well enough to tell where they belonged. "Who was my father anyway? I have never felt I had a father. All he cares about is to get another wife and another wife. I still dream to continue with my studies. I would have liked to be a social worker, but the family is hard on me, and my husband is hard on me. I have spoken to him. I told him that I want to study, to broaden my world, but he told me, 'Sit at home, take care of your children.' I must know how to educate my children, lest they become like their father. I am not the only one. All the girls in the family suffer from the same thing."

Na'ima has almost given up hope. "Unless the Jews enact a law that will improve the status of the Bedouin woman, I don't believe there will be change."

This is a core problem of the Bedouin society, and it does little to help itself. There are plenty of women's groups, but none actually goes to the families and confronts them with the real problems; they know they have little chance of influencing the patriarchal Bedouin society.

Na'ima's good friend Manal is twenty-six and unmarried. In theory, she is free to go out and study, but she, too, is a prisoner in her own home, unable to leave and study because her parents will not let her. Manal completed seven years of school. The family lives on grazing sheep. "My parents ordered me out of school so that I could go out with the sheep. When I read a newspaper, my father got really mad. He used to tear the newspaper into pieces and shout at me, 'A woman ought not to read a newspaper!'"

By now, Manal's family has grown to twenty-three people in one house, including twenty children from two mothers.

"My father's second wife is thirty-nine years old, only thirteen years older than me. We quarrel every day."

Even now, Manal spends most of her days in the field with the sheep and the other girls. Because there is no running water in the house, it is her responsibility to go with the donkey to fill the water barrels at a nearby water supply. "I, too, want to study; I want to know the world. No one listens to me. I speak to the wall. Whenever I go to town, to the clinic or to the market, I am always accompanied by men. When we watch television, and we see a couple kissing, they force me to turn my head away from the set."

Manal's most valuable asset is a cellular phone, her faithful connection with the outside world. "They don't know that I own a cellular phone. Had they known, they would have punished me. I am tired of life. Sometimes I consider committing suicide."

Sabha was thirty-four years old when she married a widower thirty years her senior. When they married in 2000, he already had four children (one married) and a grandchild at home. She married into an existing family, but has never had a family of her own. Sabha's mother died when she was fourteen. As the oldest girl in a family of nine children (with one older brother), it became her responsibility to take care of the children. Eventually, they all married before her, which subjected her to heavy pressure from her family to get married. "My brothers and sisters told me that I should get married so that I should not stay alone." They did not care that the future husband was twice her age. They only wished to marry her off.

Even the courting period was demeaning. Three months passed between their engagement and the wedding ceremony.

During those months, he came to visit only twice, and even then they were never left alone. A member of her family was always present in the room, eliminating the slightest chance that they would get to know each other before the wedding. The door was always kept open.

She thought that the old courtier would at least provide her with economic stability. "When we married, I thought I would manage somehow. I would have my own children and would live my own life, but I didn't realize how old he was." Today, her husband does not even provide her with decent living. She said that his only income is his old-age pension, the equivalent of $700 a month.

Sabha has made a fatal mistake. Eight years after the marriage, she has never loved her husband; they have no sexual relations, and he has not given her a child. At the age of forty-two, she is doomed to live with an old man, with virtually no prospects of improving her life. Nevertheless, she is afraid to get divorced, because she can no longer return to the home of her stepmother and her children. If she leaves him, she has no place to go. No one is likely to take in a forty-two-year-old divorcée.

"I hope that no one will make the same mistake. I would have preferred not to be married at all. He is a good man, but he thinks differently than me."

Luckily, Sabha works in a bride's salon and makes a modest additional income by knitting embroidery and selling it through Bedouin women's associations designed to help Bedouin women gain economic independence. This is a significant addition to the family's modest income.

None of the women we met—whether first or second wives—expressed satisfaction with their situation. At one

stage or another, they all radiated frustration. Their frustration is multiplied, because there is very little women can
do to change their status. They are caught in a prison—a
prison at home.

Polygamy is part of Bedouin tradition, but the interesting
point is that not only have they preserved the tradition, contrary to the Israeli civil codex, but also the trend has intensi-
fied in recent years—even among educated men and women.

When Sara, now forty years old, married her husband
twenty years ago, she thought she was very lucky. Radwan
was a young teacher, fresh out of college, seeming to be a
liberal and progressive young man. Her blue eyes, so con-
spicuous among Bedouin women, radiated with hope. She
believed she had a bright future. However, after twelve
years of marriage, Radwan chose to remarry. "Even if
you meet him today, you would be rather impressed. He
is very advanced and educated, a college graduate. You
would never expect a person like him to marry a second
wife. At the time, he gave me all kinds of excuses why
he needed a new wife; he explained that it was because
I brought only girls—three girls and no boy. But I knew
that the real reason was simply that he fell in love with
someone else. Although this is against the law, I did not
complain. I told myself, you have no choice but to acquiesce with your new life."

Sara has a lean face; as a pious woman, her head is covered with a yellow scarf. The new life meant radical and
painful changes, such as lonely nights, when her former
bed mate was with the new woman. Although, as a teacher,
Radwan lived on a very modest state salary, he took loans
and built his new wife a new home.

His new wife brought him four more children, but even more painful was the fact that the second wife's house became his main home. The second wife not only replaced Sara in her husband's life, but she also finds it difficult to accept that her husband still has certain obligations also toward his first wife. "He often calls me and says that he does not want any problems with his wife, so, although it's my turn, today he won't come home."

Her daughters are now fifteen, eight and six-years-old. "He comes every two weeks and barely sees the girls. They are angry at him; they often ask me whether he is really their father, because they see how much time he spends with his other children." Essentially, Sara's household has become a one-parent family. However, unlike single mothers in the Western world, there is no point in getting a divorce, because the chances are that no other man will take her. Why become a divorcée with three children when there are so many single girls available?

In the unfortunate hierarchy of Bedouin women, the status of divorced women is even lower than that of the other women. Bedouin society treats a divorcée as one who has failed in her family function, and she is often blamed for breaking up her family. She has few prospects of marrying a bachelor or a divorced man, unless he is already married or is much older.

Making the tragedy of divorce even greater for women is the fact that, because of religious law, a divorce can take place against her will, merely because the husband no longer wants her. In general, it is the husband's privilege to decide on a divorce. Although the woman can also initiate the divorce, she might need to "buy" her freedom by paying the husband a sum of money—returning her dowry, so to speak.

A divorce must be ratified by a religious judge, or *qadi*. According to Israeli law, marital affairs are subject to religious law. Thus, although the state appoints the *qadi* as head of the Muslim religious court, making him a state official like any other judge, he derives his judicial authority from the Qur'an and Islamic religious codex. The *qadi*, lawyer Dugan Mousa al-Atawneh, is yet another Bedouin authority on family affairs. However, whereas Sheikh Sami abu-Freh derives his authority from his independent standing in the town, Qadi Dugan's authority is conferred by the state.

Al-Atawneh is the only Bedouin *qadi* in the country. His office, located in an old Arab-style stone house in the old city of Beersheba, is a rare reminder of the grand old days before Israel's War of Independence, the 1948 Arab–Israeli War, when the house had been the administrative center of the Negev. Qadi Dugan al-Atawneh greeted us in his modest office, with a computer on his desk, an Israeli flag behind him, and a side door leading to the relatively small court room. It is the office in which the fates of many families are determined. Men and women (the vast majority of them Bedouin) come from all over the desert to have Qadi al-Atawneh certify marriages, rule on family disputes, and authorize divorces.

According to Israeli law, all legal matters regarding marital issues are subject to the ruling of religious courts. Just as rabbinical courts deal with marital conflicts among the Jews, the *sharia* courts rule on matters among the Muslim population.

Paradoxically, Qadi al-Atawneh is not a man of religion. He studied Hebrew and Arabic literature at the Hebrew University in Jerusalem and then received his lawyer's degree. He then practiced law in Beersheba before he was appointed *qadi* by the Justice Ministry. To qualify for this delicate position, he had to demonstrate thorough knowledge of the *sharia*.

*Qadi Dugan al-Atawneh*

During the early times of Islam, the *qadi* was a judge who ruled on all matters, criminal as well as civil, and the Bedouin still maintain a system of informal tribal law in which tribal courts rule on a wide variety of issues. Although these courts have no official and legal standing, the Bedouin often prefer to bring their cases before the tribal courts and avoid involving the state legal system. Today, the *qadi* runs the family court that deals with the Muslim population in the Negev.

Despite the fact that he is a government appointee, Qadi Dugan is generally respected by the Bedouin population, in part because of his family's status. His late father, Sheikh Mousa al-Atawneh, was a prominent sheikh in the south and a former Knesset Member who represented the socialist Mapam Party.

Unlike many of his Jewish counterparts, as a judge al-Atawneh tends to play down his importance, being direct in his discourse and eschewing pomp. When we addressed him as "Your Honor" he waved it off, saying he prefers to be addressed by his first name.

Owing perhaps to his secular education, Qadi al-Atawneh immediately conceded that, while Islam claims to be egalitarian, in fact it gives men advantages over women, especially in marriage. A basic rule of Islam requires the woman to obtain court intervention before being granted a divorce, whereas the husband has the right to divorce by simply saying *talak* (you are dismissed) three times. A man does not need to justify his wish to divorce, while a woman must convince the *qadi* that she has a good reason to divorce.

Nonetheless, the *qadi* added that, in some respects, a Muslim woman who wants a divorce is better off than a Jewish woman is. If a Jewish man refuses to divorce his wife, no divorce takes place until he consents. In the case of a Muslim couple, if the woman convinces the *qadi* that she has been mistreated in some way, the *qadi* simply grants a divorce decree, and the man must consent. On the other hand, the *qadi* told us, the man is obliged to support the woman and the children. The wife, on the other hand, has no financial obligations toward the man or her children. If the wife works, she is entitled to keep her income. As is the case for Jewish women, the Muslim divorcée is entitled to receive half the family property.

What happens to the children in divorce cases? According to Islamic law, the father (again the father) has the right to keep the children. However, Qadi Dugan said, "Just like in common law, it is the welfare of the minors that counts. The younger the child, the more likely it is that the mother will get custody. Only in rare cases, where the woman behaves improperly, does the father have the right to take the children over the mother."

Men initiate divorce more frequently than women do, because the man is the dominant member of the family, economically independent and free to do as he pleases. Islam, however, imposes a strict ban on a man leaving the first wife and children without providing sufficient support for them. Islam also forbids abandoning one's children and taking another wife. Despite such rules, however, until very recently, a divorced Bedouin woman would return to her parents' home, because men refused to pay alimony, forcing the woman to rely on her parents to feed her and her children.

## WOMEN AND ISLAM

Sheikh Sami abu-Freh of Rahat is the sixth among seven brothers and five sisters, but he was the one who became the natural leader of the family at the age of sixteen when his father died. This may have been because he was the first to finish high school, and two years ahead of schedule. He told us, "When father died, we had a family council of brothers, and we made family decisions. Usually it's the responsibility of the men in the family, but because my mother was dominant, we listened to her."

Their father had left the family with little means, and Sami considered finding work in lieu of continuing his studies. However, his mother told him, "Go on, study, I will pay." As a result, he began studies in religion at the Islamic University in Gaza. Although the university was a hotbed of Islamic fanaticism, it did not seem to affect him. In 1985, he tried to enroll at the prestigious and religiously authoritative al-Azhar University in Cairo, but they denied him admission because of his Israeli nationality. Nevertheless, he was the first Bedouin to receive a degree in Islam. Later, he moved to the other end of the cultural spectrum, studying for his B.A. in education at Ben-Gurion University in Beersheba.

*Head scarfs on display at an open-air market*

For the past twelve years, Sami has worked as a teacher, traveling to and from Hebron in the occupied West Bank to receive an M.A. in religious studies at the Islamic University in Hebron. His thesis compared Bedouin and Islamic law— the customs of the desert vs. strict Islamic *sharia*. Today, at thirty-nine, Sami is attempting to expand this issue in his studies for a doctoral degree at Amman University in Jordan. He crosses the border each week for a day of studies in the Jordanian capital.

Sheikh Sami acknowledges that, as a religion, Islam is much more liberal toward the woman than Bedouin tradition is. Moreover, Sheikh Sami argues that Islam is much more progressive than the West perceives it to be. "I know Islam inside out. I know the true Islam that we received from our Prophet Muhammad, not the Islam that is distorted in the media. I am very concerned over the situation of Islam in the world. I am saying that there is not moderate and extreme Islam; there is only one Islam."

Sami serves as the local Imam, the leader of the prayer at the al-Hilal mosque in Rahat, one of the eight Bedouin townships. "Mother is very proud of me. Now seventy-seven years old, she has never remarried, because it would have been seen as dishonoring her late husband. Mother is really special, in that she did not want to live with any of her children, but preferred to live on her own in a small one-room house. But mother is never alone. Every night, one of us children spends the night at mother's place. If one of us does not show up, she begins enquiring what happened.

"Father had been a merchant who often left the house, leaving his wife alone with the children, taking care of the children, working in the field, grazing the sheep, and even going out to the Beersheba market to sell them. She had to protect the house; thus she slept with a rifle under her bed—a dominant woman in a patriarchal society.

"One day some unknown guests showed up. However, in the best of Bedouin tradition, both father and mother interrupted their business to entertain the guests. Suddenly mother realized that, while some of the guests were having coffee, their friends tried to steal the sheep. Mother hinted to father to take care of the coffee, went to the other room, loaded her rifle with bullets, and scared away the thieves, shooting." In Bedouin culture, theft is unacceptable not only because it deprives people of their assets, but also because it shames the victims as people who can be fooled into losing their property.

The grandmother greatly enjoys the family, having about two hundred grandchildren and great-grandchildren, the result of seven sons married to ten women. Sami has two wives, one where we visited and the other at a nearby house.

Altogether, he has eleven children. This educated man of religion surprised us by saying, "I do not rule out the possibility of getting yet another wife." Sheikh Sami quoted the Qur'an: "Among His proofs is that He created for you spouses from among yourselves, in order to have tranquility and contentment with each other, and He placed in your hearts love and care towards your spouses."[15] Thus, Sami began his discourse on religion and women. "Islam does not differentiate between a man and a woman, neither in privileges nor in duties."

According to the Qur'an, the woman is the creature who dictates life for both sexes. She guides the man first as the mother, then as the wife. This is a lifelong task. "My mother often tells me, Sami, go there, or don't go there. I always listen, always obey. After all, as a mother she has a seventy-seven-year-long life experience."

Sheikh Sami's mother is the exception that proves the rule. In the absence of the father, she assumed both material and spiritual responsibilities. For example, Sami learned many Bedouin poems from her. The Bedouin are known for their poetry, much of which, unfortunately, has been lost, since much of it was never written down. "She learned poetry from her father and her grandfather. I learned it from her. I have memorized the entire hard disk of my mother."

Nevertheless, having spoken so highly of his mother, and having paid tribute to the equality of women, he immediately went on to count the differences. "Only man is in charge of the family's livelihood. The wife can work, too, but she must get her husband's approval. I gave my wife the permission to work as a teacher. If the woman and the girls observe tribal values, they can continue studies; but today in Israel, there are no appropriate conditions for girl studies, because, so far, the state has refused to set up separate educational institutions for girls. Religious Jewish girls have special *ulpanot* [girls' religious secondary schools, the equivalent of *yeshivot* for the boys], but there are no similar institutions for Muslim girls. This is why girls after fifteen do not continue studies: to avoid temptations and prevent honor killing. Family honor is one of the issues that are not to be compromised. Every town or village should have one girls' school; this would increase the number of girls going to school by at least sixty percent. We do not oppose progress and development, but we do not want modern life to take over our values, our land, and our daughters."

Islam believes in equality, but there are things that do not look equal. For example, a man has the right to divorce his wife, even against her will; a woman can do this only through a ruling of the court. Another example is the right of a woman to inherit only half of what her brothers will get from the family's legacy. "The girl will receive only half of the man, because the man has more duties," explained Qadi Dugan of the religious court in Beersheba. "He must support his family, whereas the woman has no economic obligations toward her family. Even a divorcée need not pay child support for her children."

## THE SHIP OF THE DESERT

"The ship of the desert" is a nickname for the camel, the huge, patient beast that has, for millennia, been the prime means of transportation over the vast desert sands. Alas, in modern times the camel has given way to 4x4 jeeps and pickup trucks.

Bedouin entrepreneur Farhan abu-Shleibi seems the antithesis of the slow-paced camel. Farhan moves quickly and is assertive, business-minded, and races over the desert sands in the latest four-wheel-drive jeep. His unique quality is that he transformed tradition into a business of tourist transportation. His tourism center, about twenty miles south of Beersheba, is called "The Ship of the Desert." Farhan played a special role in our desert voyage. Unlike most Bedouin men with whom we spoke, he goes along with the feminine Desert Revolution; he does not fight it. Nonetheless, he does not concede completely. He spelled out his philosophy of life shortly before a group of young German tourists gathered in the huge tent for a traditional Bedouin meal: "It's a matter of dream and will. Once one has a dream and a will, a person can do anything in life. It began as a cultural challenge. I wanted to introduce our world to the outside world. I created a place where people can meet and get to know each other; they relax, eat, and

*The Desert Ship Tourist Ranch*

enjoy themselves as I tell them stories about Bedouin life. I talk about everything, even about polygamy and marital problems. They enjoy, I enjoy—the perfect match."

Farhan has made a business out of the customary Bedouin hospitality. "Yes, we made a business out of it, and I am very proud of it. We must progress with life; we cannot march in place. We must move forward, like all other societies." Farhan's dark, curious eyes look forward and backward at the same time. He is a strong believer in progress, in pushing aside traditional obstacles to improve his own life and the life of the Bedouin community in general. He is determined that all his ten children will graduate college, but at the same time makes sure that they are well-acquainted with their Bedouin heritage. He is a calculated businessperson while still a devout Muslim who believes that, at the end of the day, providence has the final word. It is important to him that his children know what a herd is, what straw is, what a shed is, and how you lead the sheep to the shed. "It is not only a question of heritage; it is indeed a matter of leadership." Strong links to the past mean stronger bonds within the tribe—a precondition for the inevitable confrontation with the establishment.

Farhan is one of the few Bedouin entrepreneurs who have taken economic initiatives—and made it, despite all obstacles. Farhan's Ship of the Desert tourism center offers visitors from Israel and abroad comfortable lodging (not tents, but air-conditioned cabins), traditional Bedouin food served in large Bedouin tents, Bedouin music, and at dawn an exotic camel ride into nearby desert hills.

Farhan's "Ship" has become a popular destination in tours of the south, always humming with people, whether Israeli high school students on annual field trips, families with children who wish to explore off the beaten path, or tourists from overseas discovering an "extra touch" of the Holy Land. "I am devoted to my project. I believe it has an added value, not only as a tourism attraction, but I must be on the outlook all the time to make sure that it is economical; otherwise there will be no project."

As far as Farhan is concerned, there is no conflict between past tradition and present-day necessities. "We must run along with time. We must advance with the rest of the world—and this is why education is so important. Sure, I miss the past. I wish I could have gone back to the kind of life my father led, not ever looking at the watch—not only because no one owned a watch in those times, but because the concept of time was totally different. When you enjoy the present, there is no rush to seek the future, and there is no need to measure time. I wish I could have gone back in time, but there is no way to avoid progress."

Despite Farhan's flirtation with progress, as his business has developed he has moved closer to religion and sees

*Camels and guide*

no conflict between the two. Farhan believes in what he perceives as the true, authentic Islam, not fundamentalist Islam. "Had people followed strictly the religious path, the world would have been totally different." Farhan, like many young and educated Bedouin, has rejected the attempts of self-appointed "guardians" of Bedouin customs to justify cruel customs in the name of Islam.

To clarify his views, he volunteered the following comment: "Even if my own daughter goes sexually astray, I shall not be an old-time Bedouin." Meaning that Farhan would not punish his daughter, even if she opted to act in sharp contrast to traditional Bedouin values. "But things will never get that far," he added. "I educate my children so that they will never disgrace the family and the society."

Farhan's tribe, the Azazmeh, lives in the Negev plateau. The story of this tribe is an example of Israel's historic failure in the treatment of the Bedouin population. At the end of Israel's War of Independence in 1948, the tribe wanted to acquiesce with the new boss: the Jewish state. However,

Israel has avoided real responsibility and through the years has committed every possible mistake in its treatment of the Bedouin population. At first, the Israelis deported the tribe from the Negev further south to the Egyptian-controlled Sinai Peninsula. Most were eventually allowed to return to the Negev, though many others fled to neighboring Jordan. Rather than dealing with the Bedouin population as they did the massive influx of Jewish immigrants, government officials felt they had done enough by simply allowing the Bedouin to settle down. Initially, there seemed to be no problem. The Bedouin settled down with their tents and herds and no basic infrastructure of roads, electricity, or water systems, and often with no nearby schools. The Bedouin gradually felt the new situation.

In contrast to the time during the British Mandate, their movement in the Negev was governed by the military government's restrictions imposed on the entire Palestinian population after the war. Those who wished to break out of the traditional work went to Beersheba and to the newly built Jewish development towns as unskilled laborers. Worst of all, whereas they previously felt that their home was the entire desert, with no one limiting their movement, now the government restricted them to a limited region. Restrictions were justified initially by arguments for security; later, the Bedouin were restricted for geographic and demographic reasons. The government wanted the Azazmeh tamed and under control, just like the other tribes.

In the early 1970s, the government launched a lengthy process of land registration, which the Bedouin had rejected outright. They felt that the whole purpose of the process was to deprive them of their historic land rights in the Negev, while giving the land to Jewish settlers. The Azazmeh had to make do with their restricted settlement as they watched with envy as prospering kibbutzim such as the nearby Revivim and Mashabei Sadeh cultivated land that the Bedouin had perceived as their own. The Bedouin problem reflected the larger Israeli–Palestinian conflict over a stretch of land.

Like the rest of Israel's Arab population, however, the Bedouin had come to accept reality, protesting the discrimination against them but refraining from hostile actions against the state. In fact, many of the Azazmeh had volunteered for the army, offering their natural skills as trackers to monitor the infiltration of hostile Arabs into Israel.

Eventually, the Azazmeh, like the other tribes, were forced to move into government-established townships, which bore little resemblance to traditional Bedouin ways of life. Those who refused to move into the townships and instead built improvised housing wherever they pleased frequently faced government bulldozers that demolished "illegal" buildings.

Around 2005, the Negev Azazmeh numbered around six thousand people spread over about ten thousand acres. They had one elementary school, and high school students were bussed to the Bedouin township of Segev-Shalom. Social changes were very slow in coming. Most women did not go out to work; the tribe was run by a committee of four to five men. Raising sheep was still the main occupation, while others worked as laborers in Beersheba and the nearby kibbutzim, as well as those who still serve in the army as trackers. It was not until 2005 that the government adopted a

*Student outing*

plan that might meet the demands of this traditional society. It created a planned settlement designed especially for the Azazmeh tribe. Each family was offered a plot of four acres that could be used for domestic agriculture. The Azazmeh complained that it was not enough, but it was a step in the right direction.

The new township is planned on the site of Bir Hadaj, an ancient well and the original site of the tribe. In the complicated Negev conflict, there was finally an agreement between a Bedouin tribe and the government. The settlement was granted about 1,600 acres by the Israel Land Administration.

The majority of the Azazmeh, as many as ninety percent, still live in Jordan. The Azazmeh is one of the few tribes that continue to live a partially nomadic life, the reason so few of the women work outside the tribe. Many girls stay at home, not attending even a day of school. Sure, there is a law compelling education, but the state shows no interest in enforcing that law among the Bedouin population. Paradoxically, Bedouin and state interests converge in this case. Uneducated parents are happy to enlarge their free domestic labor force, while the state saves much-needed money by operating fewer classes.

Farhan abu-Shleibi is an exception. He refuses to wait for the state and the traditional Bedouin to reach agreement. Despite the importance of Bedouin heritage in his life, Farhan does not expect his son to be a shepherd; nor does he see his daughter spending the rest of her life in the kitchen. His motto: I will guide my children through the right path, but it is up to them to make the right choices. "Every person has his own way. My son and I are like brothers; I do not look down on him—particularly since he is now taller than I am. I am a much different father than my forefathers were. Parents who impose themselves on their children are losing out. One should give the children the same respect that one expects from them."

Farhan's eldest has already been designated to become a lawyer. His daughter wanted to study medicine, but in the meantime studied social welfare at Ben-Gurion University in Beersheba. "The key is education. Once people are educated, they have the motivation to make progress. The situation in Israel forces us to quit the life of the past and join modern-day life."

Yet Farhan faced a dilemma. He wanted his daughter to study, to become independent, and to adjust to the challenges of the modern world, but how far can she go on her own? We asked him whether his daughter would stick with Bedouin tradition and adopt Bedouin cultural and social norms. "I have no doubt, when she completes her studies, she will continue observing the Bedouin way of life; she will not dress up Western-style, with half her body exposed."

During his daughter's high school days, Farhan drove her to school every day. Now, however, he feels that he can let her go by bus with her brother. Even so, on days that she has early classes, he makes the point of driving her all the way to Beersheba, before beginning his own busy day. However, his wife has not yet adjusted to the idea that her daughter is traveling by bus unaccompanied by a parent. Whenever she hears of a crime in the region, she stiffens up and declares, "My daughter will not go by bus!" Then she gives in to reality and watches her children board the bus, worrying until they return home late in the evening.

The son could have received a scholarship to study medicine in Jordan, but so far the mother has vetoed the idea; the boy will not go on his own to a foreign country. The border checkpoint with Jordan is a half-day drive from Beersheba. This means that the son could leave home by sunrise and get to Amman in the early afternoon, and then come home every weekend. According to mother abu-Shleibi, however, the university is too far from her immediate reach. This is not a risk she will take, no matter what.

*Who will choose the daughter's husband?* "Neither she nor I will choose the husband. When someone comes to me and asks for her hand, I will ask her if she has any interest in him. Only if she does, will I give a positive answer."

As evening fell on "The Ship of the Desert," the workers lit a bonfire in a metal crater. A young man spread a layer of coffee beans on a pan, held it above the fire, and began shaking it to the beat of a song sung by his friend, while playing an oud, a traditional Arab stringed instrument.

Others sat by the fire and smoked a *nargilla* (a brass water-pipe). When the singer went on to the next song, the others accompanied him, clapping their hands.

Soon it was time to grind the coffee beans. One of the boys piled them in a mortar and began grinding them with a pestle, pounding with a certain rhythm. In previous times, Bedouin making their way through the desert would hear the rhythm and know that they were invited for coffee at a nearby camp. Once the coffee was ground, it was added to a pot of boiling water, cooked again, and poured into small cups.

The singing continued into the night; love songs and desert songs all lamented the good days that were no more. The music was monotonous, repeating the same tune over and over again, but its rhythm created a special air of nostalgia.

## WOMEN SEEKING EDUCATION

When Farhan abu-Shleibi was a child, he used to ride a donkey to school in the Tel-Sheva Township, making a point of never missing class. Education has always been topmost on the family's agenda. Nowadays, lamented Farhan, things are different. Education has lost its attraction. The Bedouin society does not invest enough in education, leaving large segments of its society, especially women, undereducated. Unfortunately, quite a few of the Bedouin men we met opposed the idea that girls should have equal opportunities in school. Ali a-Saraya, whom we met in his wooden hut near Arad, told us, "This is dangerous. Five years ago, we demanded separate classes for boys and girls, but the government refused, even though we were ready to pay the extra cost. Subsequently, I went to the school principal and warned him that if my girl behaves improperly, he should notify me immediately, because if anything happens to her, it is the responsibility of the teacher."

Hussein a-Rafayah was more direct: "My daughters have studied only six years, then I take them out of school. She should not go to university; a Bedouin should not allow his daughter to study. This is not the nature of the Bedouin." *What if they continue studying?* "Then they will go into areas where we don't want them to go. There are Bedouin who allow their daughters to go on with their studies, but all the Bedouin that I know, all original Bedouin, take their daughters out of school, lest she be subject to maltreatment. The son can continue studying all the way, but a daughter no." We asked whether this is really fair. *Why is it okay for boys but not for girls?* "If anything happens to her, it's a shame on the family. Only six years, and that is it. I don't know about the others, but we Bedouin of Beersheba do not allow."

Fortunately for the Bedouin, the Desert Revolution gradually has won over Hussein's own "school of thought." In 1995, only one Bedouin girl graduated from Ben-Gurion University; by 2005, the number of women graduates reached more than 500, almost twice the number of male students. Bedouin girls determined to seek an education are overcoming the shackles of tradition. However, it is not an easy task.

A Bedouin girl student may leave her home in the Bedouin tribe at seven o'clock in the morning, dressed in the traditional Bedouin dress. Two hours later, she finds herself in class at the university with boys and girls often dressed in modern, fashionable, and sometimes provocative attire. Whether she likes it or not, a Bedouin girl stands out as different from the majority of the student body. Even Shehadeh abu-Sbeit, a school principal, had his reservations. "It was a very tough decision for me to let my daughters study at the university. I was concerned that they would come back home with a Jewish boyfriend. My father and my sons objected to their studies. Only after I was assured by my daughters that they would not do anything contrary to our tradition did I give them the blessing of the road. I was lucky, but not everyone knows how to guide his children in how to distance themselves from the temptations of Western culture.

"Some girls who did not accept the tribal constraints paid heavily for their audaciousness. Their prospects to find a partner for life inside the tribe diminished. No one was likely to ask for their hand; they were considered an outcast in the family. In a way, they had ruined their own future. Anyone who cohabits with a boy before marriage finds it difficult to get married. Some women find themselves at the age of forty all alone, and only then do they recognize their mistakes. Only if I respect Bedouin tradition will I be respected; but if I show disrespect, the entire society will despise me."

Most Bedouin girls continue to fulfill the traditional home-bound duties of housekeeper, wife, and mother, but increasing numbers of girls have been permitted (by the male tribal leadership) to take advantage of opportunities for higher education and vocational training, even though they then face the temptations—and challenges—of the "outside" world. "Nowadays, the woman can study anything," said Sheikh Sami abu-Freh, the Imam of Rahat. "She can become whatever she wishes, a doctor, a lawyer, whatever." He paused for a minute and then added, "...provided, of course, that she follows Bedouin values."

The definition of Bedouin values, though, is quite vague. It is up to the master of the family to determine, whether the father, husband, or an older brother. It is up to him to decide whether the woman will work, where, at what times, and under what circumstances. He will decide whether she can work in the big city with other men, whether she will need to come home every night, and what exactly she can practice. The dilemmas are there, facing educated Bedouin women wherever they turn. As a woman doctor, can she treat male patients? As a woman lawyer, can she practice law against Bedouin customs?

Sheikh Sami will not admit it, but, in fact, he is on the defensive. He realizes that he faces strong female opposition and a steadily growing lobby of Bedouin women who will no longer blindly accept male dictation. This is the background for all the talk about the community's determination to enforce "Bedouin values."

It is not only a woman's eagerness to study, but, paradoxically, also her limitations and the man's relative freedom. Whereas a woman must report to her father, brothers, or husband wherever she goes, a young man is free to do as he pleases. Many young men prefer to go to work; others— too many—have derailed themselves and find their income in criminal activity.

Conservative Bedouin men have good reason to forbid girls studying at the university. As more girls take up higher education, girls who insist on their right to study become stronger, in turn encouraging more girls to attend school. As a result, male dominance is shrinking.

# Rebellious Women: Young Women Challenge the Men

## Dr. Rania Abedelhadi:
### The First Female Bedouin Doctor in the South

Thirty years after the first Bedouin male student graduated from medical school, Rania Abedelhadi (al-Okby) became the first Bedouin woman doctor. A gynecologist by training, many of her patients are Bedouin women, who feel more confident with her than with Jewish male doctors.

Rania was six years old when her mother took the unusual step of divorcing her husband and, as a single parent, moving to the predominantly Jewish city of Beersheba as the sole breadwinner in the family. "My father wanted to marry a second wife. He did not expect my mom to make an issue out of it. He believed that if that was his wish, since he was the man in the family, he was entitled to have his way. My mother would not accept a second wife in the house, but she had no one to support her. When a Bedouin [man] wants to marry another woman, the family still supports him. So my mother simply said no, and left home."

Rania's mother dared where others would not have, perhaps because she was not a Bedouin. She was an "import" from the Gaza Strip, back when the border between Gaza and Israel was wide open. "She did it for us. She did not want to live in a society where our father could leave us, and where we would have no choice but to depend on him. So she left everything and started to work to bring her own money home. My father did not give her any money. He said, 'Okay, you left home, so I won't take care of you or your kids.' She is a terrific woman, my mother. Sometimes we have women's talk. I ask her, 'Where did you get all this energy from?' She tells me, 'If you want something, then go for it.' She is amazing, a very strong woman, and a very powerful woman."

Despite the family crisis, Rania now knows that this decision had done her only good. "It was my mother who gave me the possibilities to fully materialize my potential; that is the secret of my success." Living most of her life in Beersheba, Rania was not raised according to Bedouin traditions. Most of her friends were Jewish. At home they spoke Arabic; outside they spoke Hebrew. At home, they were mostly Bedouin; outside they were mostly Israeli.

Rania was only sixteen when she enrolled in the medical school at Ben-Gurion University. They picked her up as an excelling student in her high school class and sent her to the university. She found her first year in school intimidating. She was the first Bedouin girl to study medicine. Nevertheless, the social reaction was overwhelmingly positive. "People encouraged me to go for it, 'We are very proud of you; we want our daughters to be doctors as well.' Everyone was expecting so much of me—my family, my friends, all the Bedouin. I thought, my God, I cannot do it. It was like being dropped into the sea without knowing how to swim.

"Although I was the first to study medicine, there were a lot of educated women before I became a doctor—social

workers, lawyers, physio-
therapists. Being educated is
not a new thing, but being a
doctor, yes."

When she set out to study
medicine, Rania knew that
this could have cost her
dearly in her private life.
"Men will not accept the fact
that I am self-confident and
independent; they will not
like me working night shifts.

*Dr. Rania Abedelhadi*

My job is very demanding,
and I would need an open-minded husband to accept this."

That was part of the reason for her decision after having
graduated from medical school in 2002. "I had a choice:
to remain here, and serve my community, be a feminist
and succeed professionally, but be lonely and still live at
home—or to have a 'normal' life." Rania chose to do her
residency in the northern city of Haifa, where she stood a
better chance of finding an Arab husband, possibly not a
Bedouin and more likely to respect her independence.

Work at the Rambam Hospital in Haifa was her first
experience working away from the Negev. "People were
surprised that an unmarried Bedouin girl would be coming to live by herself away from home. Some of the Arabs
I met admired that. Others were critical that I had left my
community."

Eventually Rania's personal hopes materialized. It was
in the north that she found her love Haled, a mechanics
engineer. They married in 2007. Unlike the south, here she

was an equal partner in laying down the rules for marriage. One of her conditions for marriage was that she would work long hours for the next few years, causing frequent absences from home.

Being so familiar with the enormous hurdles that a woman must overcome to reach her position, we asked what sort of advice she would give to her Bedouin women friends in the Negev. "Not everyone is as stubborn as I am. Everyone has a different situation. But I would like to say, 'Do whatever makes you happy.'" Then she corrected herself slightly: "Never give up, but think carefully, not to risk everything."

As a woman, both beautiful and smart, and being famously "first" in the Negev, Rania has attained a kind of celebrity status, but it is not something entirely comfortable for her. Rania's Haifa experience, she says, brought her down to earth. "People in the Negev treat me like a star. I really like it, but it is not right. I feel self-conscious. In Haifa I was just like everyone else."

In spite of herself, Rania's marriage mended her relations somewhat with her father. When her fiancé's father came to her mother's home in Beersheba, her father needed to be there, too, to give his consent to the marriage. The wedding could not take place in the absence of the father. "It was more difficult for me than for my mother. I cannot accept him in my life again. I did not invite him even for my graduation ceremony at the university, although my mom asked me to. I said, 'No, I do not want him there.' He did attend the wedding, though.

"Although I have broken traditions, there is some tradition I cannot break. Although I was raised by a mother who was brought up on non-Bedouin traditions, still, I do belong to that society; I did absorb Arab, Islamic, and Bedouin traditions. If I want to stay here, to make people listen to me or hear what I have to say, I should live or behave according to some codes. Had I wanted to break all traditions, I would have left the country, and that's it; but that would have meant that I could not bring about any change in our society."

Although Rania does not wear a traditional dress, she makes a point of putting on modest attire, to avoid unnecessary provocation. "When I go to weddings, I sometimes wear the traditional dress, a black robe covered with red flowers. The other day I went to a Bedouin wedding dressed like that. Many were surprised to see me this way, but I loved it. It is part of me, and it was my choice; no one forced on me the dress code. I am trying very hard to be modern and a Bedouin at the same time."

This convergence of two worlds has also helped Rania maintain her status as a role model among Bedouin women. They look up to her, not only as someone who has made it in the Western world, but also as one of them. The more traditional women turn to her, knowing she understands them and that they can trust her. "Generally, I like to be a role model, but sometimes I do have my difficulties. Sometimes you want to live your life the way you want to; you want to go to the discothèque; you want to go to the beach wearing a bathing suit—not bikini, mind you—but then again, people know me and I cannot behave all the time the way I want to. Sometimes, when I am abroad for example, I don't care. When I am here, especially in the Negev, I do pay extra attention to how I behave and how I talk. I have found the balance between modern life and traditional life.

"If my husband had not been supportive, I would not have been able to practice medicine. I work 286 hours a month—more than he does. Indeed, people often ask me how we can have a normal marital life, working like that. When I tell my Bedouin friends that my husband sometimes cooks for himself, they do not believe me. They say, 'Oh no, something is wrong. He actually cooks for himself?'

"I want to have four or five children, and he accepts it: 'I am married to a Bedouin woman; what can I do?' He keeps asking me, 'You are a Bedouin, and I am not, but what will our kids be?' According to our tradition, they will not be Bedouin, because their father is not a Bedouin; but I believe that in the future they will respect Bedouin tradition.

"We spoke about girls. We agreed that we would bring them up exactly as my mother had raised me. Even if they decide to leave the country and go study somewhere, I will be supportive. Certainly I will miss them, but will let them do what they want. I will want them to lead the life they want—to be happy, no matter where and how."

The first Bedouin gynecologist is certainly an asset to the Bedouin women of the Negev. Not only is it easier for them to approach a female doctor, but she is a physician who not only speaks their language, but also is well acquainted with their way of life. "Sometimes Bedouin women who don't know that I am a Bedouin first speak Hebrew. When I tell them, 'You can speak Arabic,' they get very excited: 'Oh, you are a Bedouin, so you can understand us.' Sometimes they will share with me information they would not have confided with a non-Bedouin doctor. When I examine them they say, 'Oh, you are so gentle.' They are very encouraging, very happy to see me there in the hospital."

*Can they consult you on sexual matters? Can they say, for example, that they do not feel anything during the sexual intercourse; can you do something about it?* "No, this has not yet happened. Only ten or twenty years from now will they ask me such questions. Being educated, you are more aware of your body and your life than the less educated are. When I ask, they do answer, but they do not volunteer information about their sexual life. To be honest, it is even embarrassing for me to ask delicate questions. Sometimes they tell me that they do not have sex during pregnancy, and I express surprise; but it is kind of a difficult conversation for me. They sometimes ask funny questions, such as, for example, 'I have heard that if my husband plays with my boobs I will get breast cancer, is it true?'

"A Bedouin woman goes to a gynecologist only when she is pregnant. Between pregnancies she does not go. Taking into account that an average woman has ten kids in her life, most of the time she is pregnant."

*Do Bedouin men consult their doctors on sex?* "Rarely, and when they do, they are very hesitant about it. When I was a student, I did five weeks of family medicine in a Bedouin village. One man told me, 'My friend leaves me in the middle of the way.' At first I didn't understand. It took me a couple of minutes to understand that his wife didn't satisfy him sexually."

We suggested that perhaps Rania would become the first sex therapist, though without calling it that. "Exactly, although when I told my mother that this was my intention, she asked me if I was out of my mind. I can be a gynecologist who deals with sexual problems, but I cannot be a sex therapist. For some people, the words are too upsetting, but being a gynecologist you certainly deal with sexual life."

*Do you meet women who think that there is no sex after menopause?* "Yes, most women think so. I know women who stopped having sex the minute they had menopause, and suddenly they acted more independent; they went out of the home on their own; they started smoking in public— as if they had told themselves: 'We are no longer attractive anyway, so why bother to be too modest?'

"I have no doubt, thirty or forty years from now, all will become like me now. True, being a Bedouin is a way of life; a Bedouin lives in the desert, has a tent and a camel, but just as the Jews mixed between communities and adopted their way of life while keeping their identity, the same will happen to us. It's only a matter of time."

## KAUKAB A-SAWAYYID

Kaukab a-Sawayyid, twenty-three, of the Bedouin township of Shaqib al-Salam, has challenged the traditional society from a place in which she is mostly exposed to the outside world. She is the first Bedouin female television reporter, working for a local station in the Negev. At the same time, she studies mass communications at the Sapir College near the southern town of Sderot, the target of frequent Kassam rocket attacks from the Palestinian Gaza Strip.

Her long black hair accentuates her beautiful face, prominent eyebrows, beautiful dark eyes, and a pleasant smile. She wears a fashionable pink dress. "I know that I am different from most Bedouin women—in the way I dress, I behave, I am indeed freer. Very few Bedouin women are dressed modernly. It is not that I intentionally wanted to look different. I simply went out to study, and then I realized that I am different.

"I didn't want to take the usual route of getting married at a young age and delivering children. I was determined to study. Education is a weapon in the hands of the woman. If anything happens in the family, she will have other options. Had I been married, my freedom would have been limited.

"They asked me to put on a head cover. I once tried, and I just could not stand it, so I refused to put it on again, and no one in the family had forced me otherwise. They asked and applied a little pressure, but eventually they gave in. It is my right to do what I want. I grant you that I have given up a lot by insisting on my modern looks. I know that people no longer regard me as a Bedouin, but it is their problem, not mine. I feel good with it, I am happy with myself. I am happy with the way I am being treated, despite all the criticism.

"My friends are Bedouin, Arabs from the north and Jewish girls from school. I can find friends at any place."

Because she was fortunate enough to enjoy the support of her family, we wondered whether it was easier for Kaukab than for other Bedouin girls. "I get a lot of support. My mother and my brothers support me, although I hardly have any contact with my father. He has remarried, is busy with his new family, and minds his own business; he does not interfere in my life. I am not sad; this is what gives me strength.

"I want to be married to a progressive man who will understand my work, not a closed-minded person. I like the Negev, and I like where I live. I will not live anywhere else but Shaqib al-Salam, not even Tel-Aviv. I will stay in my home town."

## MARIAM ABU-REKAYEK'S NEW HORIZONS

Mariam abu-Rekayek is one of the few Bedouin women who has dared to break down the barriers. She studied abroad, breathed the air of the wider world, and absorbed a new language, another people, and a different culture. She dared to go beyond tribal boundaries, and eventually returned home.

Mariam was fortunate in receiving her father's permission to go abroad. He entrusted her to a pair of British friends who had spent time with the tribe in Israel. In England, she studied at university, learned English, and received a degree. When she returned home, she had thought that her people would embrace her and benefit from what she had learned while away. However, for Mariam's family, that chapter of her life was closed. They perceived her overseas experience as an experience that would end with her return to Israel. They wanted the old Mariam.

Mariam had just graduated from high school when she traveled to England. Unlike her friends, who had already planned their weddings, begun university studies, or found employment, Mariam was set on fulfilling an old dream; she wished to visit London. "England, London, everyone wants to study there; it's the other world of which I have heard so much, and here was an opportunity to fulfill my dreams. It was all very new and very exciting. It was my first flight ever. Within a few hours, I found myself far away from my family. At first there was a shock. I began crying, 'What the hell am I doing here?' I was like a fish taken out of the water. I cried for three months before I finally got used to my new life."

*Mariam abu-Rekayek*
*making soap for Desert Daughter Cosmetics*

Indeed, life in England was not easy for Mariam. It was far less fun than she had expected it to be. "I lived in a place where you sit in a park and nobody knows you; nor did I know anyone. I did not even know my neighbors, and this is what I missed here. At first, I couldn't wait to come back."

Eventually, however, she not only became accustomed to life in England, she also began to appreciate what it has to offer. "I said 'Wow' about the way they do things. I learned new things about myself; I learned how to express my feelings and my ideas. What had impressed me most was British accuracy and precision. They do not compromise; they pay attention to every little detail, and this is what makes them so unique."

She took a course in macrobiotics—health methods based mostly on natural foods—and realized that her own body of knowledge on this was quite rich. She'd had an exceptionally qualified teacher, her grandmother. "Everything I know about herbs I learned from my grandma, who died three years ago when she was a hundred years old. She was the only woman among the Bedouin who was a healer. She received her knowledge from her father. I always accompanied her to the fields when she went to pick herbs. Every time I suffered from stomachache, she recommended some bitter herb, which cured me after ten minutes, even though at the beginning it was quite horrible. People are coming back to nature, and I found out that I was actually grown up in that nature."

Thus, when Mariam returned home, she plunged into studies of Bedouin natural food and medications. Her plan was to sell desert herbs and their products as a business venture. However, she found the challenge was much greater than expected.

Mariam returned home educated and experienced, but the main benefit of her stay in England was that she learned to be independent. "After three years, I came back more self-confident. The Bedouin have so many problems; I thought I would do something to help. However, as soon as I came back, I was confronted with the conflict between Western values and the conservative Bedouin society, and I was absorbed with continuous efforts to find the balance between these two worlds. True, my father really wanted me to go study abroad, but he only wanted me to pick up the knowledge, nothing else. However, as far as I was concerned, I am a human being, an individual who could not just adjust herself to the expectations of her father. I could not just read books and come back and be the same girl that I was when I left. I have seen people from a different point of view. I have changed."

Mariam has beautiful black smiling eyes and a pug nose, sensual lips, all carefully wrapped with a dark head cover— a sharp contrast to her open and free discourse. She is in her late thirties, still unmarried. She would not acquiesce with the match-making practices of the tribe. "My family wanted me to get married, but they insisted that I marry a member of the tribe, a demand that I could not accept. I insisted that I would not be married to someone I didn't choose."

At the same time, Mariam did not want to break her ties with the tribe. "I am against women who go after their heart and leave their families to marry in spite of their families. That is why I am suffering; I did not get married. I lost so many years of my life just because I was determined not to be with someone they did not want. Some of my sisters believe that it is good that I am independent. Some of them

do not think so. Not all of them are the same as me. Some
of them think that a woman should marry and raise children, and that is the good life."

We asked, "During your stay in England, did you think
you might find a British good-looking man and stay there?"
Mariam immediately replied, "Is there a good-looking
British man?" Then she added, "It did not cross my mind
for a moment that I might marry a British guy."

If Mariam were to fall in love with a non-Bedouin man
and marry him, she would probably be excommunicated
by her family and her tribe. Her conundrum is that, on
the one hand, she did not want to act against her family
and her tribe; on the other hand, she could not find her
love within the tribe. Thus, she would be left single and
frustrated. "I would never leave my family. My family is
more important than any man." Unfortunately, her family did not really appreciate her personal sacrifices. "They
don't understand the sacrifice that I made—that I did not
get married because I didn't want to dismay them; because
they wanted me to marry a man of their choice. I am still
sacrificing, every day."

The greatest assets Mariam acquired in England were her
self-confidence, assertiveness, and independence. Unable to
use them in her personal life, Mariam invested all her ener-
gies in business ideas. She would no longer obediently com-
ply with family and tribal dictates and was determined to
pursue her own path. Her main goal in life was to achieve
economic independence.

Originally she had planned to open a business that
would involve traditional medicine. "Bedouin women use
a variety of desert herbs for healing purposes. Traditional

medicine, which used to be the sole medicine, is still very popular." Eventually, she began her desert cosmetics business, a beauty shop based on desert herbs, employing traditional practice in a modern business setting. She called her business Bint a-Sahra (Daughter of the Desert). "If you had asked me ten years ago if I would ever go into the traditional vocations of Bedouin women, I would have said, 'No way!' It took me ten years to realize that one can make business out of tradition."

She launched her desert cosmetics project in 2005. By doing so, Mariam not only launched a prospering business and job opportunities for Bedouin women, but she also rescued old traditions that might have been forgotten otherwise. Moreover, she has also contributed to a "greener" world. "We are losing the planet, regardless of whether it's in America or Lagiya. We have accustomed ourselves to pizza and Coca Cola rather than enjoying what Mother Nature has to offer. So here is an opportunity to produce cosmetics that have no chemicals whatsoever, and are totally based on herbs growing in the desert."

She located her workshop in her brother's garage in the township of Lagiya. Heavy sacks of herbs fill the store room. One of the main components of her soap shop is Artemisia, known for its volatile oil. This fern-like plant feels especially comfortable in dry or semi-dry habitats. Mariam traces the origins of this shrub back to the early days of Islam. "Muhammad said this can relieve any pain," she said. "My grandma used to add them to the dough, because they were considered a preventive measure, even before anybody would suffer any pain. She used to put seven seeds in the fire against the evil eye. If someone believes in it, it

is like a self-fulfilling prophylactic. After all, the psychological effects are very important, just as important as the
physical."

Although her grandmother's heritage was paramount in
developing her business, Mariam also took a formal course
on desert herbs at a local college. Mariam considered the
formulae for her soaps a professional secret, inherited from
her grandmother and known only to her and her aunts.
"Unfortunately we don't have many young people who
know this, and the old people are dying. This knowledge is
going to disappear if we do not take care. It's sad, because
we are losing so many traditional things, all natural things
about life."

Mariam gathers her herbs from the fields, dries them,
and then immerses them in cooked olive oil for twenty days
or so. Once the soap ingots are dry, she cuts them into individual soap bars. Mariam pointed to a black soap, made of
black cumin oil, patchouli oil, and lavender. "I use the soap
to treat acne and skin diseases such as psoriasis, eczema,
allergy to commercial soaps, and for beauty, to help face
and body. It wasn't easy for me to turn this knowledge into
business, because it was new; I am the first one to do it."

In her determination to succeed, Mariam even ignored
the wishes of her father. "My dad didn't want me to have
my own business, because I am single, and that made things
more difficult for me. Had I been married and my husband
would have agreed, it would have been easier for society
to accept. My family is unhappy that I do a business that
involves meetings with men, and that makes it difficult for
me to go out on my own to business meetings. Had I been
married, my family would not care where I was going. They

*Mariam gathering herbs for her cosmetics*

do not even give me the credit that I can cope with my dreams, but I am determined to show them that it will succeed. It's quite difficult, but if I succeed, others will learn from me and follow suit."

We asked, "What about your friends?"

"I don't really have close friends, because when you are in a bad time you don't have friends. It is difficult to get good friends, because when you get in a bad situation, no one wants to hear from you. Besides, most of my friends shared the view that I would not make it. I used to feel awful about it when my friends and my family didn't believe in what I was doing, but now I trust myself that whatever is not achieved today will be attainable tomorrow."

We wanted to know, "What do Bedouin men think of Bedouin women who develop their own careers?"

"In the real Bedouin tradition, the woman was the other half of the man. Men and women worked together in the field, but now Bedouin men are more aggressive toward women than they used to be. Now they think the only place for the woman is at home. The main reason for this change is the change in the work patterns of the men. They no longer work their own land; they go to work in the factory, but they want to keep the woman at home."

"You are a professional woman who builds a business," we said. "Do you really think there are men in your society who would adjust to a modern way of life for a Bedouin woman and marry her?"

"Of course there are, but they are not easy to find."

As we were talking to Mariam, a local TV crew with a young Bedouin woman reporter came to interview Mariam. She was dressed in jeans with a sleeveless shirt. When we saw this, we asked Mariam, "What do you say when you see this reporter dressed like a modern Western woman?"

"I don't want to interfere in the affairs of others, but I don't want Bedouin women to appear as she does. But at the same time, if that is what she chooses, it is her decision to be what she wants to be. But if she is ashamed to look like a Bedouin, then I do not like it. I want the Bedouin woman to be dressed in a distinct Bedouin dress. At the end of the day, regardless of what she wears, outsiders will treat her as a Bedouin."

We had met Mariam in her office, and now she suddenly interrupted the conversation, "Excuse me, but I must go inside to pray." This energetic businessperson took time out for an intimate dialogue with the Almighty, away from her guests. However, she did not miss the opportunity for a feminist comment about men. "This is why the woman does not go to the mosque to pray. Men need the company of other men to gather the energy to pray, but a woman's energy is strong enough to pray alone; that shows how powerful we are."

Mariam's perception of Islam seems different from that of most Bedouin men. "In Islam, we have the right to choose. Why should I not have that right as a Bedouin woman? The Bedouin are Muslims. Why do they not practice Islamic law? Why are they sticking to more conservative practices?

"In the past, women and men shared everything, but now it's different. We are in a new situation in which we do not have the same rights and we are not equal. I need my brother's permission to go to town; this is how it is done. Why? I cannot answer for something that was decided generations ago. My challenge is not to find the answer but rather how to cope with it.

"In the past, men and women worked together in the fields; the entire family was together all day long. They used to care for each other. The husband need not worry about his wife, because she was right there next to him, all day long. What has changed in recent years is that the man no longer works in the field, but goes out to work as a wage earner, leaving his wife alone at home. When he is away from her, he keeps asking himself what she is doing in his absence. Thus he wants to ensure his control over his wife by proxy, either through his parents or through his brothers.

"Actually, come to think of it, it is not only a matter of control over the woman. The woman is very important for the Bedouin men; she is half of the family. They protect the women more than control them.

We said, "You are doing a very difficult balancing act. On the one hand, you want progress, and on the other, you are committed to Bedouin tradition."

"A few years ago I, too, shared the view that the two were mutually exclusive, but now I realize that the secret is to take the good of both worlds, put them together, and it will work. I think it is possible. Being a Bedouin does not mean that one cannot be a revolutionary, that one cannot be a success story, although I grant you that it is quite difficult; it's not easy."

*Will you ever have children?* "In our society, it is very important for a woman to have children, but I don't know yet if I will have children—maybe yes, maybe no, but it's not something that I am killing myself for. It is more important for me to be independent than to be married and have ten children. To be independent means that I say what I want to say, and I follow my thinking and my beliefs."

*Will you consider becoming a second wife?* "I used to say no, but now I am at an age in which I may say yes. The rate of unmarried women in the Bedouin society is incredible, so I cannot be against this practice if it can solve the problem of so many girls."

Mariam knows polygamy from home. Her father has two wives who brought him thirteen daughters and five boys. He has six brothers from four different mothers.

The conversation was interrupted again as a group of local travel agents entered the shop. They came at the initiative of the tourism ministry's division of internal tourism to put the Bedouin villages on Israel's tourism map. Ironically, although Mariam was still struggling to receive the recognition of her own society, the Israeli establishment was already encouraging her to move forward.

Mariam abu-Rekayek now uses ancient traditions to blaze new trails. At present, Mariam's market is local, but her dream is to grow large enough to export her products overseas. "I am selling a bit here, a bit there, friends and family. I have not yet linked my business to a marketing service. I am thinking to sell it in Israel, but I dream to sell our products also in America, Europe, and Japan." As we concluded our conversation at Mariam's shop, she took time out of her busy schedule and invited us to join her in the field to collect herbs. Out there, she blossomed, and the desert seemed to blossom with her. "When I go to the desert, rarely do I see an herb that I don't know." She moved from one dull-looking plant to another, praising their qualities. "This is good for the digestive system, and this one works wonders as a pain killer. And this plant smoothes the skin more effectively than any commercial cosmetics."

The herbs serve both as seasonings and as natural medications. The thorny burnet, for example, is used widely to treat diabetic patients. The plant is also used to treat stomachaches, toothaches, gingivitis, and external inflammation and as a tranquilizer.

"Desert plants are different from any other plants in the world; they are unique in that they live in a very tough environment, and they are fighting for their life—just like me."

She carefully selected the herbs, identifying each of them by name and cutting them with small shears. Every now and then she sniffed or bit an herb to make sure she picked the right one as the basket filled.

"This is how we Bedouin do it. I smell or taste the plant to recognize what family it belongs to. Sometimes I do not know the plant, and this is my way of making acquaintance with the plant. When I use a plant for my cosmetics workshop, I don't just pull it out. I only use the part of the

*Mariam hosting a group of tour guides*

plant that serves my purpose. All the rest I leave, because I believe it is my responsibility to take care of this plant for future use. In a way, this is my motto in life—to take and to give at the same time. If you are generous, you will always get back what you have given others, be it plants or human beings."

When she goes out to the outside world—which is now limited to the town of Beersheba, since she rarely goes north to Tel-Aviv—Mariam does not conceal her Bedouin identity. Rather she is proud of it. She walks in downtown Beersheba with a black head cover, which does not take away from her beautiful face, accentuating the rosy cheeks, the bright dark eyes, and the sensuous lips.

She walks confidently in the midst of the predominantly Jewish town, as if she is a natural part of the human landscape, although Jewish women her age pass by dressed in miniskirts or tight jeans. She stands out in her brown jacket on top of a beige sweater and her long brown checkered dress. "I am trying not to lose my Bedouin identity, but at the same time I want to live my life as I choose. It is so difficult for me, particularly as a woman. I must respect the honor of the family, its identity, and at the same time I am asking for my rights. I must respect what the family respects. Honor means many things; it means that I should not lie, that I should not give in to my sexual needs. In general it means that I must adhere to the values of my society."

We observed that it seemed as though she was paying a heavy personal and social price for her actions. "You always pay for your choices in life. I am at peace with myself for having chosen to be alone and independent; this way the Mariams of the next generation will have it easier to be independent. I and other women like me suffer to make it easier for them."

*Can the Bedouin society survive the changes or will it disappear?* "This is what I am concerned about, that after ten or twenty years we will lose our identity. I am not at all sure that my kids or my nephews will look, think, and act like Bedouin. I think we are losing our identity partly because we are taking from the West not the good things. I ask myself this question all the time, and I see too much black. Only if we take the good things from the West, while not losing our identity and keeping our tradition, will we be a successful society."

As we were about to leave Miriam's shop, Dr. Ruth wanted to give her a word of personal advice: "I understand how difficult it is for you, but don't give up on having a family. You can do both the soap *and* the family, but you must find the partner who will support you."

*Lakiya Negev Weaving*

For a moment, we stopped being outside observers. "Look at me," said Dr. Ruth. "I lost both my parents when I was ten years old because of Hitler, who killed my entire family. So for me, family is very important. I have two children, and that makes me very proud. I managed to develop my career *and* have my family. Therefore, I would like to see you married. I do not want to see someone like you saying to herself some day, 'Too bad I didn't get married.' I believe you can do it all. It is very difficult, but it's possible."

## KHADRA A-SAN'A:
### A "BEDOUIN FLIGHT ATTENDANT"?

Whereas Mariám is more or less still at the dreaming stage, Khadra a-Sana'a, also from the village of Lagiya, is already active with her Sidri association, a group of six women who formed a weaving enterprise that offers them the opportunity to work at home, making a living and achieving a

*Khadra a-San'a with Ruth*

measure of independence away from the overarching rule of the men. Sidri specializes in weaving carpets of sheep wool.

Khadra told us, "At the beginning the men opposed the project; they wanted the women to go to the field, cook, weave the tent. They opposed, because they did not want the woman to come out of the home, but we outsmarted them. Most of our work is done at home, at the women's leisure. So, the husbands have lost their excuses against our work."

Each worker takes home a specific carpet design, a miniature replica that she begins to weave. All that the woman needs is a loom and other members of the family to help out. As she works at the loom, her sisters and daughters sit with her, chatting and laughing, making work an enjoyable family enterprise. Khadra pays home visits to help the women with their work. Later, the woven carpets are colorfully dyed and placed for sale at the Sidri store. Each woman receives a monthly salary. Any additional profits go toward developing the enterprise.

It is fascinating to see how Bedouin women have managed to combine the tradition of raising sheep with making money. Almost every Bedouin keeps sheep at home. The women sheer the sheep to obtain their raw material for weaving the carpets. The sheep are an important element in the life of a Bedouin. They provide milk, wool, and eventually delicious meat, though the meat is usually served only on festive occasions.

"My husband is happy with my professional progress. I worked even before I got married. When I met my husband, he did not object to my work. That is why I didn't have any problems."

Unlike Mariam, Khadra is very hopeful about the prospects of the Bedouin woman's self-fulfillment. "In the future, we shall see the Bedouin woman working in everything, even as a flight attendant. We can make progress and keep tradition at the same time."

### YUSRA ABU-SIAM

The "competing" weaving center in the village of Lagiya is at the home of Yusra abu-Siam. As she sits at the loom, weaving her Bedouin carpets, she is surrounded by women friends chattering about everything from the wedding of their neighbor to the latest developments in the peace process. Although most of them barely finished elementary school, they listen to the news on the radio and often watch television. They stay current.

This center weaves carpets and other goods from sheep's wool. "The logic of our weaving center is that women can work at home. They receive some $35 per square meter of weaving, which takes about four to five hours of work."

The center sells a carpet of three by three meters for $750. After paying for the labor of the women, the money helps expand the center.

"At first the men opposed; they stuck to the old ways, when the woman either stayed at home or went out with the sheep." The men were concerned that, if the women went out to work, rumor would spread that the husband could not take care of her. Yusra had worked before she married her husband, and, once married, her husband respected her choice to work.

If Dr. Rania, Mariam, and women like them are the leaders of the Desert Revolution, these women working at home are the rank and file. The success of this revolution depends on them.

## WOMEN AS COMMUNITY LEADERS

A Bedouin flight attendant? Unlike Khadra a-Sana'a, most Bedouin women activists are far less hopeful. They are convinced that the only way to advance the rights of Bedouin women is through public and political pressure. Indeed, in recent years, educated Bedouin women have established several women's rights groups in the Negev, struggling uphill against a male-dominated society. They argue that men should welcome their way, because they do not challenge old traditions, but connect to them. They want to reestablish the role of the woman as a full partner in the Bedouin home, just like old times.

Jalila al-Krinawi, twenty-six, is one such community leader. She works for Shatil, the empowerment and training center in the south, developed by the New Israel Fund. Jalila is the Bedouin women's empowerment project coordinator. She organizes three courses for young Bedouin women. The subjects are how to lead a healthy way of life for young mothers; promoting education in Bedouin homes; and a course on sexual education—although, for social and political reasons, it is called "family planning."

"It is still difficult for me to come to a school principal and tell him what's going on in that course—for the simple

*Graduation ceremony of a women's household training course*

reason that the Bedouin father will never agree to have his daughter study about the male sex."

Unlike most of the Bedouin women we met, Jalila spoke warmly of her father, and not just as a father, but also as a good friend. She considered her eighty-five-year-old father to be her lucky strike in life. Unlike most Bedouin men, he gave his daughter the green light to study. "My father never went to school, but he encouraged me to study." She has completed her first degree and plans to study law and teach Hebrew literature.

Sheikh Suleiman al-Krinawi, Jalila's father, is one of the more influential sheikhs in his town. He allowed Jalila to move freely from her home in Rahat to Beersheba, and even to wear modern attire, though she makes a point of covering her head with a scarf. She also drives her own car. Her seven brothers and one sister also gave her the blessing of the road.

Jalila's family is the exception. Contrary to the usual Bedouin male approach to women, when Jalila was a child her father spoke of the equality of women and the husband's duty to respect his wife. "He understood from early on that, if a Bedouin man gives credit to his spouse, she will lift him to the skies." Despite his liberal views, Sheikh Suleiman did take a second wife, apparently determined to give her equal rights in the family. This is why Jalila lives with her mother, despite her close relations with her father.

Jalila wears a fashionable long grey dress, with a long-sleeved white shirt—despite the heat of the summer. Under her white headscarf, she reveals beautiful black smiling eyes, a pug nose, and rather sensual lips. She is an attractive young woman and undoubtedly broke many hearts, but remains unmarried. "They have been trying to match me with boys ever since I was eighteen, but I liked no one. In our society some ninety percent of marriages are arranged by the father. This is not the case with me. I want to choose"—within traditional frameworks, of course. She will not go with a young man to the movies or sit with him in a café, but she will go to her father and tell him if she finds someone she likes.

"I want my career, I will not agree that the family will come and force me to marry someone with lesser education than mine. I have seen many good-looking guys, but when I see the environment he came from and the way he treats his sisters, I see the true picture. Sure, we have many lawyers, psychologists, and doctors, but many of them are still quite primitive when it comes to the treatment of women. My friend married a psychologist, and suddenly she disappeared from the university. Why? The Bedouin man will do his utmost to keep the woman under his reign. Why do men believe that the restrictions of tradition apply only to women? Another friend, who completed her university studies in spite of her family, ran away to the U.S.A."

We met Jalila on a hot summer day. She was at a ceremony to celebrate the end of two courses designed to upgrade the household skills of Bedouin women. One course promoted a healthy lifestyle, offered in cooperation with the medical faculty at Ben-Gurion University in Beersheba. The other involved a dialogue on education, designed to improve communication between the Bedouin home and the school. According to Shatil statistics, about seventy percent of the successes in school was linked directly to the way the family approached education. As Bedouin women become more educated and empowered, they develop unpredictable expectations. Moreover, they find it increasingly difficult to find men willing to meet their expectations. Jalila compared educated Bedouin women to the status of educated black women in the U.S. There, too, she believes, black men prefer women with lesser education.

There is a catch: "Bedouin women now have greater expectations, but they cannot fulfill them without prior consent of the men in their families. Sometimes the revolution begins at home."

## RAWIYA ABU-RABI'A

"Are men ready to give up control?" Attorney Rawiya abu-Rabi'a is skeptical. She is twenty-seven and fresh out of law school. "So far, men have not given up control for the simple reason that the present state of affairs is easy for them, so why bother?" The consequences are therefore inevitable: "They won't give up control until they are forced to."

Rawiya offered to take us for a walk through the Bedouin market in Beersheba. It is a market where men still sell sheep as they have for generations. Nevertheless, it bears little resemblance to what it used to be. In the past, the Bedouin market was a festive place for selling and buying livestock and commercial goods, whereas today the livestock market is limited to a small compound at the southern edge of the city. In the past, most of the retail trade took place there, but today it is limited to minor transactions, since most Bedouin buy their meat at the local supermarket. The Bedouin used to move their livestock through the desert for many days; now they transport their sheep and goats on pickup trucks. They stand with a few sheep and goats and haggle. Some do not even bother to take them off the trucks. Once a transaction is concluded, the animals are simply carried from the seller's truck to the buyer's car.

The old market is a thing of the past, but the atmosphere remains. One still hears the bleating animals, the angry haggling, and the dominance of men who still wear traditional Bedouin attire. "These are the remnants of old customs," Rawiya told us. "In a way, it is only a symbol for our determination to hold onto things of the past. Although we have cars, modern dress, and cell phones, we still have traditional customs, and people want to hold onto these things."

An old man wearing traditional Bedouin clothing is followed by his wife dressed in black, with her face mostly covered. Some women have even adopted the stricter dress codes imported by conservative Iranian and Afghan Muslims, by which a woman's entire face is covered so that strange men cannot see them at all.

"Don't misjudge the situation," explained Rawiya. "Although the man leads the way and the wife drags behind him, this is not necessarily the situation at home; it doesn't necessarily indicate her role in the family. She might still have a significant role."

*Ruth with Rawiya*

The livestock market takes place shortly after sunrise. Later in the day, another market pops up nearby. It is a modern open-air market, with fruit and vegetable stands as well as a variety of other goods, from children's toys to work tools. Unlike the livestock market, this market is no longer predominantly Bedouin, nor is it dominated by men. Jewish women in shorts mingle with Bedouin women covered from head to toe. Russian immigrants compete with the Bedouin venders; Hebrew, Russian, and Arabic mix in a cosmopolitan setting. "In the past, the market was pure Bedouin," said Rawiya, "but today it is a market that has lost its uniqueness. One positive development—some Bedouin women can come to the market unescorted, whereas in the past they could not come here without a chaperone, some kind of a man escort from the family."

Rawiya is not yet married, and she owns a car and moves about freely. No one tells her what to do, neither in her family nor in her tribe. She is her own woman. In her blue jeans and fashionable short-sleeved shirt, Rawiya looks much like the beautiful women of any Western community. However, in the Negev and the humming Bedouin market, she stands out as different. "Where is she from?" asked one elderly Bedouin curiously.

"She is from here, a Bedouin," we volunteered.

"She is not a Bedouin," said the man categorically.

"Yes, she is," we corrected him.

"No, she is not; a Bedouin girl cannot dress like this."

Rawiya comes from a very educated family. Her father, Dr. Yunis abu-Rabi'a, was the first Bedouin physician. "It was a very special home. My mother is a non-Bedouin, an Arab from the northern town of Nazareth. As my father had worked in the local hospital, I grew up in Beersheba, adopting a nontraditional, modern way of life. When you look at me from the outside, wearing jeans, you tell yourself, 'What a modern girl,' but the truth is that I live in between worlds. Thirty or forty years ago, this was a traditional society. People do not turn modern overnight."

It seems as though Rawiya could live in both worlds and enjoy the benefits of modern Western society while respecting her traditional society. Unfortunately, she told us, this is impossible. "Sooner or later, I will need to make a choice between the modern and the traditional path."

A few days later, we escorted Rawiya to Rahat for a discussion with a group of women on women's rights. She has no illusions; Rawiya knows that the odds are against them and that the struggle for equal rights in Bedouin society is a lonely battle, because the conservative elements of Bedouin society are still very strong. Nevertheless, she believes that her only real choice is to continue the Sisyphean work, since

*Rawiya speaks with women about their rights*

the alternative means continuation of the status quo and men's exploitation of women.

Rawiya faced a barrage of questions. The women wanted to know how they could obtain their rights and the legal means available to take legal action against their husbands. Rawiya suggested that, in most cases, they stood a better chance of maintaining their rights by appealing to the state family courts rather than to the Muslim religious *sharia* court. She also explained that it would require courage to face their tribe, since they would be perceived as breaking tribal tradition. "It's a very complicated process," said Rawiya. "Those women may sometimes appear confident, but many of them have had some sort of a traumatic experience with their husbands. Some did not get a divorce even though their husbands had left them, because they felt that as divorced women they would be less respected."

Some spoke of their fear of making waves by introducing changes in their society. They explained that it was difficult for them to make a change without family support. "I fear my husband will divorce me," said one woman. "He can easily send me back to my parents' home. Husbands can get away with anything; it's as if women have no rights whatsoever." She was in her mid-thirties and wearing an embroidered Bedouin dress with a white headscarf. Her pretty full face expressed fear; but more, it expressed despair and lack of hope that things will change.

Rawiya said, "I feel very obligated—and fortunate—to do this work. As an educated person, I have the privilege to help these women and give them some hope. I want them to feel that, if they can overcome their fears and despair, they can change their life. I know that it will not happen just like that; it will take time, but I want them to look up to me as a role model, so that they say to themselves: Okay, if she can do it, than I can do it."

## MONA AL-HABANEIN

Some women do not wait for a role model, perhaps because they can no longer stand the situation. Such women take command and ride the waves, no matter how high they are. One of them is Mona al-Habanein, thirty-seven, of the township of Rahat. Mona has prominent black eyes in a round face under the black head scarf, a curving nose, and smiling lips. Her mischievous eyes seem to say, *Never mind the traditional dress that covers my femininity; just look into my eyes; see the woman in them and listen to her story.*

Mona is divorced and learned the hard way when enough is enough. She learned that, to end the man's absolute rule, a woman must fight. Mona had set out on her painful campaign after her traumatic divorce. She had to leave behind

WOMEN AS COMMUNITY LEADERS 155

four of her six children with their father, who was reluctant to give her any child support. Now, as a consequence of her experience, instead of going to the religious court, which tends to side with the husband, she encourages divorcées to seek help in the state court, where they stand a better chance. For the first time in their lives, these women have learned that it should not be assumed that the wife must leave the home—that they can remain in the home with the children and that the husband must leave. Moreover, if the husband does not pay alimony and child support, they can receive the money from social security, while the state sues the husband for ignoring court orders.

Mona believes that the Desert Revolution is not just for young, educated women, but that it should also speak for the "simple women, because they are the ones who are really suffering." Mona points at herself as one of those women. She completed high school but feels that she was deprived of the right to enrich her world in the way that other women had succeeded in doing, in the way that men are free to choose. Mona concluded her high school studies in July 1988. By October, she had already married her cousin, to whom she had been engaged for the past year. She had not wanted to get married. She felt too young, and there were many inviting opportunities out there.

As early as 1988, boys and girls were already studying together in the same classroom. However, although they shared classes, there was very little communication between boys and girls. Some separation was institutional; some was natural. Boys and girls sat in the same class, but they never shared a desk. During breaks, boys and girls assembled separately and avoided contact. They barely spoke to one another, lest someone suspect "immoral behavior." The more expressive eye contact replaced verbal contact.

"Of course there were secret loves, but they needed to be kept secret. A friend of mine fell in love with a boy, so she bought herself a necklace with his initial. Sometimes we used to send each other secret letters, but that was really rather risky because, when the teacher got hold of such letters, those who had written them could be thrown out of school, not to mention the trouble that awaited them at home. When I was sixteen someone sent me a letter that he liked me. I was surprised, and just like any girl who gets such a letter I was happy. I tore the letter to pieces and reprimanded him for doing that, just as I was expected to do, but inside I admired him for having braved the pressures of society and having written me that letter."

Nor were the teachers much help. They lived in a constant state of fear of the families, the society, and the state. As Arab civil servants employed by the Jewish state, they were afraid to offend anyone politically. Thus, contrary to the practice in Jewish schools, there was no freedom of speech. "We were not allowed to speak about our national identity; neither could we discuss politics, commemorate Arab national events such as *al Nakba* [the Arabic term for the Palestinian defeat in Israel's 1948 War of Independence] and Land Day. It was absolutely forbidden. Not because they did not want the children to know, but because the teachers feared they might lose their jobs. I had never understood why on the one hand I needed to study the First Testament, but yet I was not taught the history of the Palestinian people."

Mona's younger sister was thrown out of school in the tenth grade because she had written "Palestine" on the class wall. "Even our father was afraid to protest and demand that my sister could return to school. She did not even understand what she did. She said she had done it because her friend told her to, but my father was afraid to stir waves. So she never returned to school. She sat at home doing nothing, feeling sorry for herself. This is all part of the general rule: As a woman, you cannot be yourself; you cannot talk about politics; you cannot express your love; you must keep everything inside, and you turn out a torn person."

Mona was the sixth child in a family of twelve children. Thus, there was no rush to marry her off. However, at seventeen years old, she was promised to a boy her age, her first cousin. "He came to me and told me that he loved me and wanted to marry me. I told him that I did not feel that I was ripe for marriage, that I wanted to build myself, and that I wanted to study social work or psychology. He promised me that I will continue studies after the wedding, a promise he had never intended to keep. Despite my objection, he then went on to my mother—his aunt—and she, in turn, tried to convince me to say 'yes.' I tried to put up a fight. She told me that I should first get married, be under the protection of a husband, and then go study. She did not quite understand me, because none of my older brothers had studied. Her strongest argument in favor of marriage was that I was going against tradition by refusing to marry my cousin. So I gave in to destiny and I got married.

"Wedding night was an unpleasant surprise. Before we went to bed they told us that two women would wait outside to make sure that the wedding was consummated, and this only made things worse. No one had prepared me for marriage. I barely had any previous knowledge on sexual relations. Neither my mother nor my sisters had spoken to me about it. It was taboo. I was fourteen when I got my first period, and I did not understand what happened. It came to me as a surprise. I cried, but I had no one to turn to and ask for explanations. Even if we girls talked among us about the subject, it was always jokingly, as if it did not really affect us, as if we would not have to cope with it some day. Even after we got married, I was afraid to discuss sex with my husband. Luckily, I could read Hebrew, so my main source of information of sex was women's magazines. At least my daughters have benefited, because—unlike my mother—I talk to my daughters and explain to them the facts of life."

It is difficult for Western observers to understand how teen-age girls in Bedouin communities can be detached from modern life? After all, they watch television. However, watching TV in some Bedouin homes involves certain restrictions. Girls are banned from watching certain shows. A girl who watches a program in the presence of her father would not dare watch anything that is not approved by him.

Mona's young husband worked as a bookkeeper at a local firm. When he returned home in the early afternoon, dinner would be waiting for him. However, his wife was not really sure how to cope with their life as a couple. "Although we gradually got to know each other, I was still stuck in a permanent state of dilemma. I was sharing my life with a person I did not love, with whom I had nothing in common. As far as I was concerned, it was an artificial relationship."

After four years of marriage, problems came onto the surface. "I was twenty-two when I began to work as a substitute school teacher. He agreed, because he saw the benefit of another income in the family budget. Whenever I raised the issue of going out to study, he objected, saying that we could not afford it, which actually was true. On top of everything, members of his family began to mix into our life and incite him against me."

Their fragile relations soon affected both families. When Mona's father had a dispute with her husband's siblings, the husband sided with his family and directed his rage at Mona. She reacted similarly when she heard bad things about her family. Relations between both families deteriorated to the degree that, as a result, a family dispute arose that had nothing to do with the couple, ending with a cruel compromise: Mona and her husband would divorce, and she would give up her children and any rights to their common property.

"I protested. I said 'no,' but no one was there to help me. My husband took sides with his family against me. My daughter was only forty days old when we came before the religious court. I objected to the divorce, but when the *qadi* asked me if I agreed to the divorce, I said 'yes,' because I had no choice. Had I said 'no,' I would have endangered my life. This is not simple."

Four children were given to the custody of the husband, while a boy and a girl remained with her. Having nowhere else to go, Mona returned to her parents' home. "I was really depressed, I neglected myself, I lived on tranquilizers. They ruined my life. My husband soon remarried. I saw my husband and kids live with another woman in my own home, but what hurt me most was the loss of the children at a young age. Ten years have passed. Even today, when I think that they are away from me, it hurts so much. Even now, when he takes the two children to stay with him, I am afraid that he will not let them come back. He lets me see the other four whenever he feels like it, sometimes twice a week, sometimes once a month. My only consolation is my fifteen-year-old son who maintains daily telephone contact with me.

"Although the children would have preferred to stay with me, they understand that they must stay with the father. They have grown accustomed to living with their new family, with their step-mother and their step-siblings, but what is going to happen in a few years, when they grow up? I still live with my parents, but I feel so lonesome. I cannot have any intimate contacts with other men. I am a reborn virgin. I am only thirty-eight but, because of my limitations as a woman in the Bedouin society, I feel as if I am three hundred years old. Sure, theoretically I could remarry, but only as a second wife. I even turned down one courtier who was single. There was one person that I liked, but he said that he would not take me with the kids."

After a while at her parents' home, Mona realized that she would not spend the rest of her life doing nothing and feeling sorry for herself. She was determined to pull herself out of her misery; she began writing poems and sought volunteer work that would keep her busy. As a result, she volunteered for a year with the Yadid human rights association. "Indeed, the place has strengthened me, but it particularly opened my eyes to recognize the problems of the Bedouin women. There are women who suffer from acute violence; others are not allowed to take one step out of the home without the escort of a husband or a brother. There are women who are sexually harassed and cannot open their mouths. There are men who look liberal from the outside, but at home they can rape the wife and beat her up." As much as she suffered, she now realized that other women were suffering much more, and she met them as a matter of daily routine—single women, widows, and divorced women who were beaten or even raped by their husband, with no one there to listen to their cries. "I wanted to listen; I wouldn't leave a woman until I saw happiness in her face. I often went home crying."

It was then that she decided to set up her own women's organization, the Princess of the Desert, to advance women's rights and offer women an open door where someone would listen to their problems and try to help. "Most women's organizations deal with economic hardships, but very few deal with the body and the soul, and that is where we come in." The association has been active for six years. She sits in her small office at the Rahat municipality building, meeting with the women and listening to their plight. "Those stories depressed me. I felt I needed to help, but the initial reactions were negative. People saw in me a rebellious woman who opened the eyes of other women. I introduced the women to their rights. I showed them ways other than those determined by the men. What is most difficult is to see how much women are not aware of their rights. There were men who wanted to shut down my association, because suddenly divorced women came and demanded alimony and other rights." Nevertheless, so far they had failed. Now Mona plans to expand her activities. Next stop, politics.

## THE DESERT REVOLUTION:
## PROSPECTS AND PERILS

On a sidewalk of a busy street in downtown Beersheba, a young man walks, dressed in jeans and a fashionable T-shirt, a mobile phone hanging around his neck. He is accompanied by his young wife, covered from head to toe in a black dress. Even her eyes are covered in an Afghan-style *burka*.

For the time being, this is the dominant picture among the Bedouin of the Negev. They have daily contact with the urban environment, in which most of the men work. As a result, the men have adjusted to that environment and enjoy its benefits. However, women have not yet attained such freedom. Nonetheless, some Bedouin men are gradually realizing that times are changing and beginning to accept the new reality. At some point, the women of the Negev will no longer acquiesce to their status as second-class citizens. Moreover, some Bedouin men—alas, still a minority—support the Bedouin women's demand for change.

Yussuf is the owner of the private TV station that employed Kaukab as a reporter. On the face of it, there is no difference between himself and any young Israeli. He grants his wife full freedom to do and go wherever she wishes. Even so, Yussuf does not want to transgress the framework of religion and tradition. Thus, even he puts limits on his wife's movements.

"My wife knows what the red line is, and my daughters will never bring boyfriends home; neither will she ever dress up provocatively. If my daughter wants to study in London, she can do it, but only if I or my brother or her husband escorts her; she cannot go on her own. It is a very narrow line; with all due respect, it is very difficult to observe this line between progress and tradition. I do not think that this is an indication of inequality. Even Western women are not totally equal, because the woman is different from the man; she has different innate characteristics. However, I grant you there is much room for improvement of women's status among the Bedouin."

The key to change, Yussuf conceded, is education. One needs a revolution in education. Bedouin girls should have the option to study all the way to the university, and the standard of Bedouin schools should be improved radically.

"I want a radical change in the approach to education. I would like to see in each home several educated people, I would like to see twenty or thirty Bedouin professors. The time of the camel is over. This is the time of hi-tech. Every poor society can make progress in arts and science. We are on the way to finding the solution to progress and yet, at the same time, to preserving our unique values. If we become a Western society, then what have we done?"

So where does the Desert Revolution stand? Unfortunately, it is at the very beginning stage. The Negev has scores of associations for Bedouin women, calling for women's empowerment and offering open doors to Bedouin women in trouble. Public figures such as Dr. Rania Abedelhadi and lawyer Rawiya abu-Rabi'a are excellent role models, but for now they stay out of politics. They cannot act as influential community leaders who can initiate significant changes in the status of the women in this part of the region. There are thousands of female "soldiers" ready to engage in the revolution, but they lack leadership and those who can lead them at this critical stage in the life of the Negev Bedouin.

Mona al-Habanein, the head of the Princess of the Desert Association may be such a leader. She may turn out to be the desert princess who will begin the change. She is certainly ready and hopeful. Mona feels that the state of the Bedouin woman is so low that things can only get better. "I know for sure that one day this boiling pot will blow up, but who will lead the revolution—our intellectual elite or the simple, angry women? The women who will lead the struggle are those who suffer most. A woman who lives on butter and honey will do very little."

Mona talks and sounds like a politician and may very well become one. She toys with an idea: to compile a list of women who will run in the upcoming municipal elections. She has already assembled a number of women and discussed the idea. It would present male politicians of her town with a new reality—a list that could upset the absolute male domination in the town. It would make the Desert Revolution not a distant option, but an existing political reality. "Only women who suffer will launch the revolution. Destruction will lead to reconstruction," Mona told us.

For a moment, she looked as if the task she had undertaken was too heavy. Is she, along with her friends, strong enough to lead the Desert Revolution? She is not sure, but she is aiming high. One step was the list of women to run in the municipal elections. Mona is a leader of this initiative. "First we told the women, 'Use your right and vote. Don't succumb to the practice in which fathers, husbands, and brothers take the identity card of the woman and vote in her place.'"

The next step was to entertain the idea of creating a women's party. They are still hesitant. They look around for help, but do not really know where to find it. If they apply to one of the parties, they may become captives of that party; if they do not, their initiative might only fail. The prospects exist. A women's list could hit the jackpot and reshuffle the political cards. "If we succeed, the entire Bedouin scene will look different."

One of the most significant hindrances to a revolution for women is the plight of the whole Bedouin community in the Negev. Male leaders must direct the resources of the Bedouin population toward improving the overall conditions for the Bedouin population in Israel. As long as that fragile community suffers poverty, unemployment, crime, poor education, and conflict with the state over land, the advancement of the women's situation will remain difficult. Ultimately, the delicate relations between the State of Israel and its Bedouin citizens may be absorbed into the whole Arab–Israeli conflict. If solutions are not found soon, and if no real dialogue takes place, the conflict might become part of the wider conflict.

Some forecasts are rather gloomy. As early as 2004, Israeli intelligence experts predicted that a Bedouin Intifada, a violent uprising in the Negev, was only a matter of time.[16] Some are convinced that, in fact, a Bedouin Intifada is imminent—the inevitable consequence of a government policy that has failed to find a common language with this Arab population, which for years has shown no overt hostility toward the Jewish state. Indeed, many of its young men serve in the Israeli military.

By contrast, other experts such as Dr. Erez Tzefadia of Sapir College in the Negev have ruled out a Bedouin revolution. "They are a peaceful community that does not believe in violence as a means of achieving political goals," wrote Tzefadia.[17] He warned, however, "The Jews perceive the Bedouin as potential rebels. Like a vicious circle, oppression and discrimination make the oppressor fear revolt, and the fear of revolt—whose signs are detected in property and illegal construction offences—in turn nourish oppression and discrimination."

All this could have been prevented. If the state had treated the Bedouin with respect, promoting education, employment, and proper housing, the whole Bedouin population would have progressed in a very different direction. On the other hand, if the relationship with the Bedouin population improves, if the people had the sense that they were finally on track for a Bedouin renaissance, the women's revolution would have a much better chance. In the absence of a framework within the establishment with which they can identify, however, the Bedouin seek other means, the most accessible of which is the Islamic Movement, the most radical organization among Israel's Arabs and the least likely to advance a genuine partnership with the Jewish state.

What should Israel do? It needs to begin real dialogue with whoever is willing to talk, including the association of the unrecognized villages and the Islamic Movement. Dr.

Thabet abu-Ras, a geopolitical expert, is deeply involved in the affairs of the Bedouin people. He has suggested that the state give the Bedouin problem the same resources it has given the immigration issue. In other words, the Bedouin Arab citizens should be just as dear to the state as are new Jewish immigrants.

The Regional Council for Unrecognized Villages in the Negev, an unofficial body of Bedouin activists, is one of the strongest advocates for the Bedouin population. In numerous publications, it has defined the major steps needed to find a just solution to the Bedouin of the Negev, including:

- Creation of a wide range of settlement choices for a mixed urban–rural Bedouin population.
- Adjusting the settlement pattern to accommodate the Bedouin society's character and culture by recognizing the tribal identification and affiliation with the newly built community.
- Reaching a final settlement on the land registration process.
- Creating a sound economic basis for the Bedouin communities, decreasing dependence on their Jewish neighbors as employers, and taking full advantage of local labor supply.
- Creating a self-run Bedouin administration that would deal with the needs of the smaller communities, while creating local municipalities in the townships. This would allow local cooperation with the planning and development process in Bedouin communities.
- Creating a five-year plan for improving the local infrastructure and services to diminish the historic gap between Bedouin and neighboring Jewish settlements.

If the government had dealt with the problems, many of the problems that Bedouin communities face could have been averted. Moreover, the problems are increasing. Nevertheless, it is not too late; anything done immediately will prevent problems in the future. It is a question of who will take up the challenge. A bureaucratic solution is doubtful, since the Israeli establishment is at odds within itself about the right course of action.

Thus, the Bedouin are caught between a rock and a hard place. They stand between Israel's efforts to concentrate them in townships and the poor socioeconomic conditions that arise as a result. The townships lack basic infrastructure and municipal services, as well as access to employment. Nevertheless, the Bedouin are banned from living outside the townships, because the state wishes to end "sporadic" Bedouin settlements and what it perceives as chaos in the Negev.

Most of the problems that the Bedouin face have arisen because of dramatic cultural and social differences. The gap is simply too wide. The Bedouin claim most of the Negev; the state claims that there is no legal foundation for such a claim. As early as the mid-1970s, the state began their "land settlement" program, a lengthy process of putting order into land registration in the south. However, well into the first decade of the twenty-first century, it has seen no significant progress.

Author Tzur Sheizaf recently wrote a novel, predicting that the present Bedouin situation in Israel would lead to a Bedouin revolution by 2009. Whether his prediction is accurate or not, the Bedouin issue is a demographic, social, and political time bomb that no one really understands or has the courage to dismantle.

The situation for Bedouin woman is indicative of the Bedouin issue in general. Bedouin men suffer because they, too, live in an impossible situation. Israeli Arabs in general feel like second-class citizens, whereas Bedouin Arabs experience themselves as third class. The men seek recognition and respect, but they are often unemployed and undereducated. They are forced to seek respect within their own communities and families. As a result, men feel that their interests are best served by forcing women to stay at home and remain subservient, and to hell with the woman's welfare. Thus, the women lose out. A male-dominated Bedouin society is intolerable for progressive women, and unless they enjoy the support of their fathers and brothers, they fight a very lonely battle.

One cannot overestimate the possibilities that such changes imply. A successful dialogue between the State of Israel and the Bedouin could serve as a model for an overall solution of the Arab–Israeli conflict. Moreover, a successful Bedouin women's revolution could lead to similar progress for the entire population of women in the Middle East.

# NOTES

1. Julie Cwikel & Nurit Barak, *The Health and Welfare of Bedouin Arab Women in the Negev*, Ben-Gurion University of the Negev, June, 2002, p. 12.

2. A. Al-Krenawi & J. R. Graham, "Divorce Among Muslim Arab Women in Israel," *Journal of Divorce and Remarriage*, 29 (3/4), pp. 103–119, 1998.

3. This section is based largely on Jenny Bahou & Ivette Nessim, "Foodways of the Bedouins in the Negev," Online Teaching and Learning, University of Maryland, December 15, 1998.

4. A. Al-Krenawi & J. R. Graham, op. cit.

5. "Ritual Female Genital Surgery among Bedouin in Israel," *Archives of Sexual Behavior,* vol. 24, no. 5, October 1995, pp. 571–575.

6. Julie Cwikel & Nurit Barak, op. cit, p. 59.

7. Rida Muhammad Rashid, *Tafsir al-Qur'an al_hakim*, vol. 4, p. 349.

8. Julie Cwikel & Nurit Barak, op. cit., p. 20.

9. *Haaretz*, March 27, 2008.

10. Arnon Sofer, "The Bedouin in Israel: Geographic Aspects in 2007," *Ofakim Ba'Geographia* (Horizons in Geography), Haifa University, 68–69 (2007), pp. 224–236.

11. *Haaretz*, March 27, 2008.

12. Ibid.

13. This part relied on Ksenia Svetlova's investigative report "Two Wives," published in the *Jerusalem Post*, July 8, 2005.

14. Julie Cwikel & Nurit Barak, op. cit., p. 58.

15. "The Romans," verses 20–21.

16. *Haaretz*, May 24, 2004.

17. Ibid., February 6, 2008.

DR. RUTH K. WESTHEIMER is best known for her pioneering work in the field of media psychology, specifically sex. However, her doctorate from Columbia University is in the Interdisciplinary Study of the Family, and she has created several books and documentary films investigating the family. The documentary on which the book is based, *Shifting Sands,* is airing on PBS stations across the country. Lantern Books also published *The Olive and the Tree: The Secret Strength of the Druze* (2007), her previous book based on the documentary of the same title. Dr. Ruth teaches seminars at both Yale and Princeton. She is working on several new books to add to her collection of works on sex. *Shifting Sands* is her thirty-sixth book.

GIL SEDAN has worked for the past thirty years as the Arab Affairs correspondent of Israel Television Channel One and the Jewish Telegraphic Agency Jerusalem bureau. He has filmed numerous documentaries on the Arab minority in Israel, most recently on the Arab town of Umm al-Fahem, controlled by the Islamic Movement. Sedan was editor and host of the Arabesque Middle East television magazine, the only bilingual (Hebrew–Arabic) regional program. Sedan majored in Middle East History at Tel-Aviv University, and earned an M.A. in journalism from the University of Missouri. He guest lectured on Middle East history at the University of Florida (2000) and presently teaches television reporting at two colleges in northern Israel. Gil is also coauthor of *The Olive and the Tree: The Secret Strength of the Druze* with Dr. Ruth.